ASIA–PACIFIC TRADE FACILITATION REPORT 2024

PROMOTING SUSTAINABILITY AND RESILIENCE IN GLOBAL VALUE CHAINS

APRIL 2024

ESCAP
Economic and Social Commission
for Asia and the Pacific

ADB

Contents

Tables, Figures, and Boxes

DIGITAL AND SUSTAINABLE TRADE FACILITATION

TABLES

FIGURES

BOXES

THEME CHAPTER: PROMOTING SUSTAINABILITY AND RESILIENCE IN GLOBAL VALUE CHAINS

TABLES

FIGURES

BOXES

Foreword

By Armida Salsiah Alisjahbana, ESCAP

Reducing trade costs is imperative to ensure the active engagement of economies in regional and global value chains. Such efforts are crucial for harnessing trade as a pivotal catalyst for both economic growth and sustainable development. Geopolitical conflicts disrupting global supply chains and heightened inflation contributing to increased trade costs continue to impede international trade. Recognizing these challenges, it is clear that trade facilitation plays a key role in advancing sustainable development by fostering more efficient and transparent trade procedures, enhancing the resilience of global supply chains, and reducing overall trade costs.

The *Asia-Pacific Trade Facilitation Report 2024* underscores the unwavering commitment of countries in the region to cultivate a seamless and efficient trading environment, despite these challenges. This commitment is evidenced by their concerted efforts to simplify and digitalize formalities in international trade, as highlighted in the 2023 UN Global Survey on Digital and Sustainable Trade Facilitation.

The report showcases the progressive efforts made by countries in the region in digitalizing their trade procedures, although there is still room for improvement. The potential benefits of advancing cross-border paperless trade are clear; reversing the trend of escalating trade costs through enhanced efficiency achieved by streamlined and digital processes. The report also indicates that further acceleration of digital trade facilitation implementation could cut average trade costs in the region by approximately 11%. Moreover, the Framework Agreement on Facilitation of Cross-Border Paperless Trade in Asia and the Pacific, a United Nations treaty that entered into force in early 2021 and currently has 13 Parties from the region, plays a pivotal role. As a dedicated, inclusive, and capacity-building intergovernmental platform, the treaty can support countries in the region in advancing trade digitalization.

Furthermore, the report sheds light on the commendable progress made by countries in Asia and the Pacific in implementing sustainable trade facilitation measures, particularly initiatives supporting women in trade facilitation. However, while the adoption of these measures is promising, it lags behind the implementation of general measures included in the World Trade Organization Trade Facilitation Agreement. Further advancements are essential to extend support to small and medium-sized enterprises, women traders and the agricultural sector, ensuring inclusive and sustainable trade becomes a tangible reality.

I hope this report will foster a forward-looking perspective on trade facilitation among countries and development partners, bolster evidence-based public policies, strengthen the exchange of good practices, and identify emerging needs for capacity-building and technical assistance. Such collaborative endeavors can support countries in Asia and the Pacific toward inclusive and sustainable trade.

Armida Salsiah Alisjahbana
Under-Secretary-General of the United Nations and Executive Secretary
United Nations Economic and Social Commission for Asia and the Pacific

Foreword

By Yingming Yang, ADB

The coronavirus disease (COVID-19) pandemic exposed the vulnerability of supply chains and the importance of mitigating shocks and disruptions. As the pandemic recedes, however, much economic uncertainty lingers due to inward-looking trade policies, geopolitical conflicts, and intensifying climate change.

These factors have important implications for trade and global value chains (GVCs) in Asia and the Pacific. GVCs in many sectors are highly complex, involving many suppliers across numerous countries. This system has enabled firms to reduce costs, achieve scale economies, and benefit consumers globally. It has also facilitated participation in trade and underpinned productivity growth in many economies in the region.

While greenhouse gas emissions from production have grown in the region, partly reflecting fast economic growth and the region's industrial structure relying more on manufacturing, emissions from trade have increased even faster due to expanding global and regional production networks. At the same time, the region is becoming increasingly exposed to adverse impacts of climate change. Extreme weather events are likely to increase, which may disrupt supply chains, while environmental regulations may impose compliance costs on top of existing trade costs.

The *Asia-Pacific Trade Facilitation Report 2024* highlights the increasingly important role of trade facilitation in ensuring more resilient and green supply chains. Trade facilitation can boost GVC sustainability and resilience through improved customs procedures, enhanced cross-border data sharing, and increased transparency. This helps identify bottlenecks, reduces border wait times, and supports sustainable sourcing. It also fosters international partnerships, enhances logistics and supply agility, and aids small and medium-sized enterprises. Technology plays a key role in risk management and ensuring smooth supply chain operations. Additionally, harmonizing standards and easier access to trade finance bolsters financial stability in GVCs.

The report emphasizes that digitalization in trade can be effective in enhancing global supply chain resilience and sustainability. Digitalization, transport facilitation, and cross-border paperless trade are essential in reducing trade costs and reaping the benefits of GVCs. Despite high implementation rates in various trade facilitation reforms, progress in paperless trade has been slow. This highlights the need for region-wide initiatives, including the Framework Agreement on Facilitation of Cross-Border Paperless Trade in Asia and the Pacific, and similar agreements.

I am confident that this report will broaden understanding of the challenges we face to ensure greener and more resilient global supply chains and trade, and the actions needed to promote trade facilitation to achieve these goals.

Yingming Yang
Vice-President (South, Central and West Asia)
Asian Development Bank

Acknowledgments

This publication was jointly prepared by the Regional Cooperation and Integration Division (ERCI) of the Economic Research and Development Impact Department of the Asian Development Bank (ADB), and the Trade, Investment and Innovation Division (TIID) of the United Nations Economic and Social Commission for Asia and the Pacific (ESCAP). The overall production of the publication was supported by ADB's Technical Assistance Support Fund 6668: Support for Forward-Looking Trade Facilitation Measures in Asia and the Pacific.

Jong Woo Kang, director of ERCI, ADB and Yann Duval, chief of the Trade Policy and Facilitation Section at TIID, ESCAP led the preparation of this publication.

The chapter on Digital and Sustainable Trade Facilitation was provided by ESCAP. The contributing authors include Chorthip Utoktham, Silvère Dernouh, Matthieu Levasseur, and Soo Hyun Kim, who provided the analysis of new data for countries in Asia and the Pacific, collected as part of the United Nations Global Survey on Digital and Sustainable Trade Facilitation 2023. The authors are grateful to Jie Wei from the United Nations Economic Commission for Europe for supporting data collection in Central Asian countries.

The theme chapter on Promoting Sustainability and Resilience in Global Value Chains was provided by ADB. Contributing authors include Kijin Kim, Benjamin Endriga, and Zemma Ardaniel. A background paper was provided by Ben Shepherd. The publication benefited from comments and suggestions provided by ADB's regional departments and the Climate Change and Sustainable Development Department.

Kijin Kim coordinated overall production assisted by Aleli Rosario. Eric Van Zant edited the manuscript. Eric Mercado created the cover design. Joseph Manglicmot did the layout and typesetting. Tuesday Soriano proofread the material with assistance from Zemma Ardaniel, Carol Ongchangco, and Aleli Rosario. Support for printing and publishing this report was provided by the Printing Services Unit of ADB's Corporate Services Department and by the Publishing team of the Department of Communications and Knowledge Management.

Abbreviations

ADB	Asian Development Bank
ASEAN	Association of Southeast Asian Nations
ASYCUDA	Automated System for Customs Data
CAREC	Central Asia Regional Economic Cooperation
CO_2	carbon dioxide
COVID-19	coronavirus disease
DSTF	Digital and Sustainable Trade Facilitation
ESCAP	Economic and Social Commission for Asia and the Pacific
ESG	environmental, social, and governance
EV	electric vehicle
FTA	free trade agreement
GHG	greenhouse gas
GVC	global value chain
LDC	least developed country
LLDC	landlocked developing country
OECD	Organisation for Economic Co-operation and Development
PRC	People's Republic of China
SIDS	small island developing states
SMEs	small and medium-sized enterprises
TFA	Trade Facilitation Agreement
TFI	trade facilitation indicator
WTO	World Trade Organization

Highlights

◼ | Digital and Sustainable Trade Facilitation

Trade costs are on the rise and volatile due to global supply chain disruption, but trade facilitation implementation could mitigate these challenges. Geopolitical conflicts have caused further disruption to global supply chains, and high inflation is contributing to increased trade costs and uncertainty. This has put additional pressure on already high trade costs in Asia and the Pacific. According to the latest data from the United Nations (UN) Economic and Social Commission for Asia and the Pacific (ESCAP)–World Bank Trade Cost Database, South Asia has the highest intraregional trade costs in Asia and the Pacific. On the other hand, East Asia has the lowest intraregional trade costs among all Asia and Pacific subregions, followed by the Association of Southeast Asian Nations (ASEAN) subregion. The Russian Federation and Central Asia, as well as the Pacific, also have high intra- and extra-regional trade costs.

The 2023 UN Global Survey on Digital and Sustainable Trade Facilitation shows continued progress in streamlining and digitalizing trade processes in Asia and the Pacific. The UN Global Survey reveals that the regional average implementation rate for 31 "general" and "digital" trade facilitation measures stands at 67% in 2023. Based on 46 common countries, an increase of 3 percentage points was observed in 2023, compared with 2021. However, implementation rates vary greatly between subregions in the region. Australia and New Zealand showed the highest implementation rates (97%) followed by East Asia (83%), Southeast Asia (76%), and the Russian Federation and Central Asia (74%). Particularly, noteworthy progress is observed in the Russian Federation and Central Asia, with an 8 percentage points increase between 2021 and 2023. On the other hand, some subregions are still catching up, with South Asia, Iran, and Türkiye (65%) and the Pacific (42%) subregions showing the two lowest subregional implementation rates.

Building on measures outlined in the World Trade Organization (WTO) Trade Facilitation Agreement (TFA), countries in Asia and the Pacific would benefit greatly from trade digitalization. The 2023 UN Global Survey indicates that the WTO TFA related measures are generally well-implemented in the region, with implementation rates typically exceeding 75%. On the other hand, despite continual advancement in establishing and enhancing their national paperless systems for exchanging trade-related data and documents, countries in the region continue to face challenges implementing cross-border paperless trade as shown by the average implementation rate of only 42%. The implementation of digital trade facilitation measures beyond the commitments stipulated in the WTO TFA could yield a reduction of approximately 11% in trade costs.
To expedite progress, collaborative efforts are imperative among regional stakeholders to establish a regulatory framework and technical protocols conducive to the seamless electronic exchange of trade-related data and documents across borders and throughout the international supply chain. The Framework Agreement on Facilitation of Cross-Border Paperless Trade in Asia and the Pacific can serve as a dedicated, inclusive, and capacity-building intergovernmental platform to support countries toward realizing trade digitalization objectives in the Asia and Pacific region.

Trade facilitation strategies should be formulated more comprehensively and inclusively, recognizing the pivotal role of groups with special needs in fostering sustainable and inclusive development. Despite modest progress, the implementation of sustainable trade facilitation measures, particularly those tailored for small and medium-sized enterprises (SMEs) and women, remains low, with average implementation rates of 43% and 42%, respectively. Conversely, the implementation of agricultural trade facilitation has a relatively higher implementation rate of 62%. Embracing and further developing measures tailored to support SMEs and women is essential, fostering inclusive and sustainable trade facilitation mechanisms that contribute to the Sustainable Development Goals (SDGs). Additionally, the report underscores a strong positive correlation between the digital and sustainable dimensions of trade facilitation, suggesting synergetic opportunities through concurrent enhancements in both dimensions.

Overall Implementation of Trade Facilitation Measures in 47 Asia and Pacific Countries

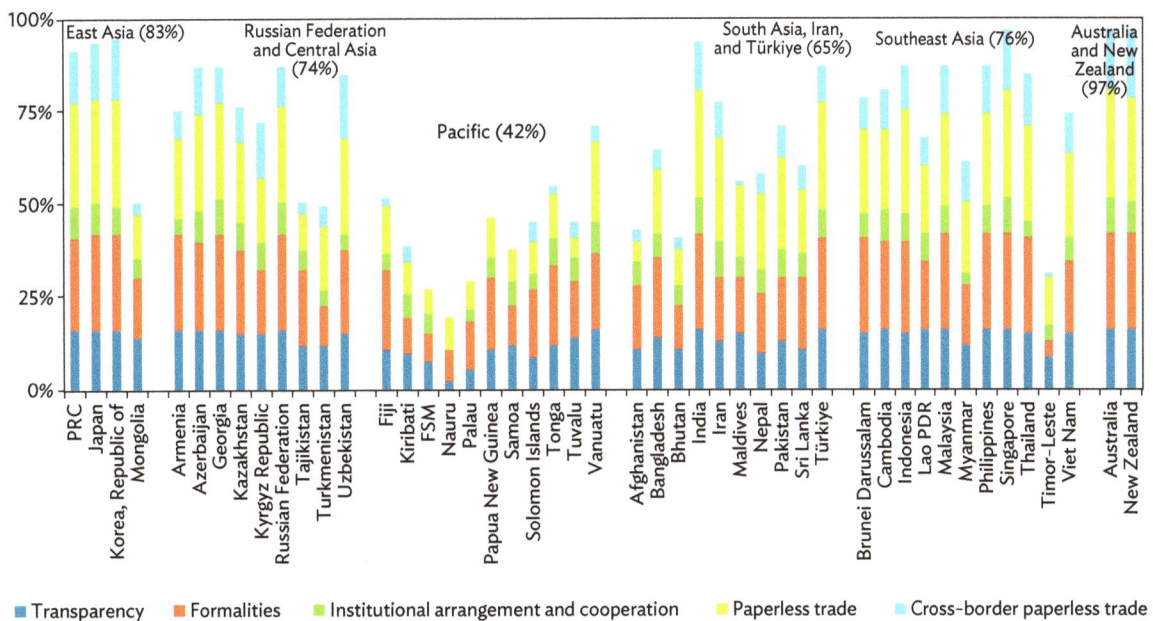

FSM = Federated States of Micronesia, Lao PDR = Lao People's Democratic Republic, PRC = People's Republic of China.

Note: Among the 60 measures surveyed across the United Nations regional commissions, three measures including electronic submission of sea cargo manifests, alignment of working days and hours with neighboring countries at border crossings, and alignment of formalities and procedures with neighboring countries at border crossings are excluded when calculating the overall score as they are not relevant to all countries surveyed. Four transit facilitation measures are also excluded for the same reason. Additionally, sustainable trade facilitation and other trade facilitation are excluded as these newly added groups of measures were not included in the earlier surveys, for comparison.

Source: United Nations (UN). UN Global Survey on Digital and Sustainable Trade Facilitation. 2023 Survey results at untfsurvey.org.

◼ | Theme Chapter: Promoting Sustainability and Resilience in Global Value Chains

Global value chains–trade facilitation nexus

Asia and the Pacific has been a key player in global value chains (GVCs), i.e., the fragmentation of production across countries. Including activities such as design, production, marketing, distribution, and support to the final consumer, GVCs often feature narrowly specialized—in sectors, products, tasks, and activities—and frequent movement of intermediate goods and services across borders during production. The region's GVC trade climbed from $621 billion in 2000 to about $3.6 trillion in 2022, and its global share of GVC trade from 24% to 30% over the same period.

The importance of trade facilitation is increasingly evident in GVC trade dynamics. GVCs often involve multiple border crossings, potentially leading to increased trade costs through higher tariffs, border taxes, transportation, insurance expenses, and unaligned regulatory measures. Moreover, trade in intermediate goods typically demands greater time sensitivity compared to final goods. The activities facilitating trade significantly impact various stages of GVCs. Paperless trade procedures and information and communication technology infrastructure improve speed, accuracy, and transparency in border clearance, while institutional cooperation reinforces these benefits. Transportation is critical in stages that involve the physical movement of goods. Overall, enhanced trade facilitation, especially through digitalization, broadens and increases GVC trade.

Rising need to address sustainability and resilience in GVCs

Asia's carbon dioxide (CO_2) emissions from trade have grown more rapidly than those from production. Globally, CO_2 emissions from production increased by 60%, but emissions from trade doubled during 1995–2018. In Asia and the Pacific, CO_2 emissions from production rose 150% and from exports by 250% in the same period. This trend has seen the region's share of CO_2 emissions from exports relative to production-based emissions rise from 22% in 1995 to 31% in 2018. The region has consistently been a net exporter of CO_2 emissions, while the rest of the world has been a net importer. In GVC trade, exports of intermediates have been more carbon-intensive than exports of final goods. This indicates a significant opportunity for decarbonization efforts to more effectively target trade in intermediates.

The resilience of global supply chains was significantly tested and disrupted in the pandemic. Drastic lockdowns and mobility restrictions hurt trade and supply chains. At its onset, the pandemic starting in 2020 exposed the vulnerabilities of globalization and global supply chains, particularly in sectors such as personal protective equipment, food, and agricultural products. This situation led to a rethinking of the geographical concentration of supply chains. In late 2021 and early 2022, the ongoing pandemic, coupled with the Russian invasion of Ukraine, further slowed global supply chains and shipments, while consumer demand began to recover. Indicators suggest an increase in supply chain pressure following longer waiting times for container ships at ports and rising shipping costs. These developments highlight the importance of an integrated approach to trade and transport facilitation to improve supply chain resilience.

Trade facilitation for sustainability and resilience of GVCs

Trade facilitation measures reinforce GVC sustainability and resilience. Improved customs procedures and enhanced cross-border information sharing enhance transparency, which helps identify bottlenecks and measures to reduce wait-times at borders. They also help companies sustainably source materials, in turn improving sustainability and resilience. In addition, trade facilitation eases firms' access to international partnerships and contributes to logistics and supply management agility via simplified procedures and faster border crossings.

GVCs in many sectors are highly complex, involving a huge number of suppliers—including small and medium-sized enterprises (SMEs)—spread across several countries. Technology is not only vital to manage risk and deal with unforeseen shocks, but also to ensure the smooth day-to-day operation of the supply chain, in particular the timely delivery of goods. Harmonizing standards and regulations simplifies compliance, and facilitating easier access to trade finance strengthens the financial stability of businesses within GVCs.

In particular, securing greater transparency in supply chains is key to making GVCs sustainable and resilient, as it encourages best practices and helps to identify vulnerabilities. Such monitoring provides information on the components of products, their parts and materials, and how they are transformed throughout the value chain. This information helps businesses and policymakers identify bottlenecks and the appropriate responses. Moreover, greater traceability helps to verify sustainability claims and incentivizes firms to be more transparent with consumers and stakeholders. It enables the pinpointing of locations and suppliers that integrate environmental upgrading into their operations.

Among trade facilitation measures, digitalization holds potential to substantially improve traceability and in turn mitigate carbon emissions and enhance resilience in GVCs. This underscores the need for an accelerated transition toward digital trade facilitation using the latest technologies. For instance, big data and analytics can analyze vast volumes of information to identify inefficiencies, while artificial intelligence and machine learning enable process automation. Blockchain technology provides a secure database for real-time tracking of goods. When prioritizing sustainability and resilience-enhancing trade facilitation measures, such as paperless trade, the implementation of trade facilitation in Southeast Asia is found to be more conducive to the adoption of green practices. These practices include the use of digital tools like single windows, which also strengthen GVC resilience.

Factors Affecting Global Value Chain Resilience and Sustainability, and Trade Facilitation-Related Factors

GVC = global value chain.

Note: Orange circles represent factors with high relevance to trade facilitation.

Source: Authors.

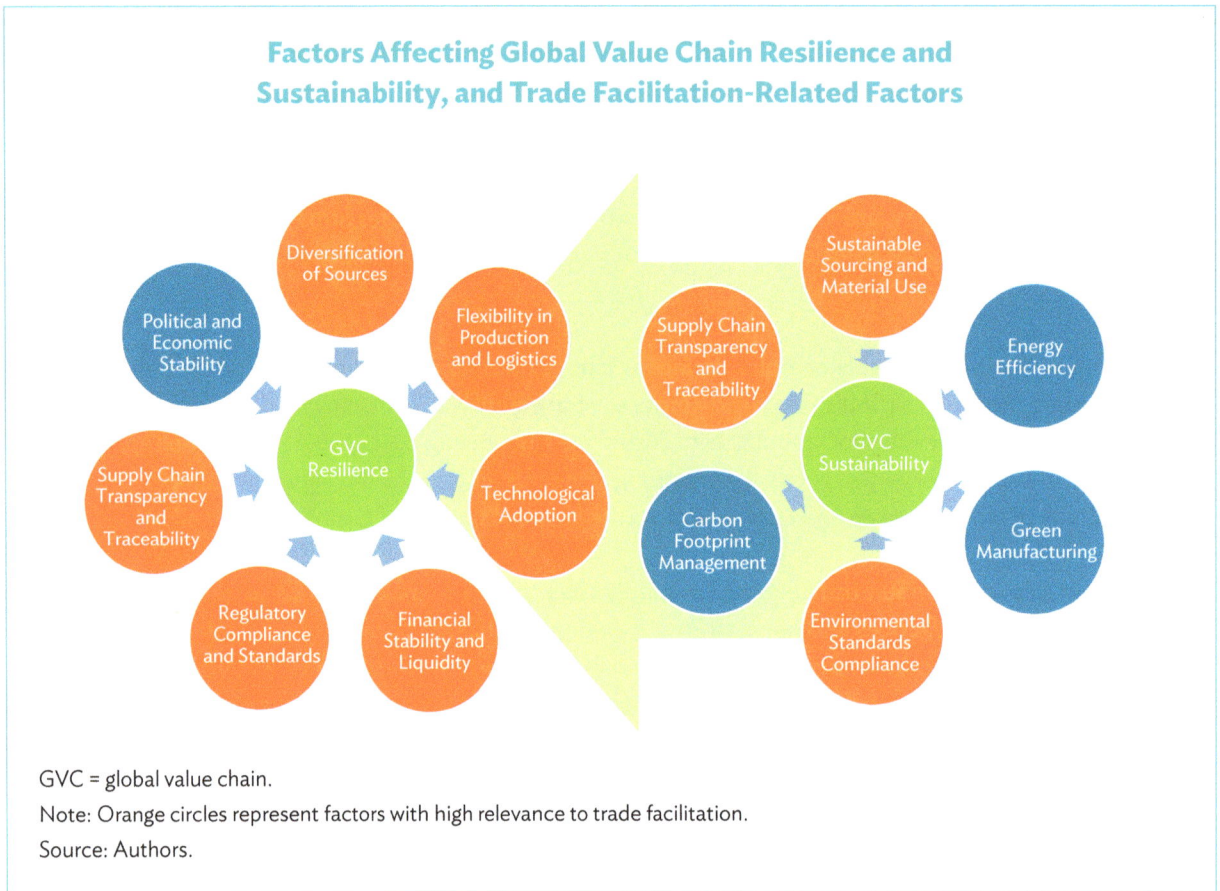

Policy implications

Despite their benefits for the region, GVCs now face a mix of challenges and opportunities. Decarbonization, for example, presents a significant challenge, as it may increase costs for carbon-intensive sectors within GVCs, which are designed to minimize supply chain expenses. However, the growing emphasis on environmental policy is shifting demand toward environmental goods like electric vehicles and renewable energy products. These products are already being produced through GVCs in Asia and the Pacific, presenting commercial opportunities. To capitalize on these, policies that support the free movement of environmental goods and services across borders are crucial.

The World Trade Organization (WTO) Trade Facilitation Agreement (TFA) remains a key benchmark for countries to enhance their trade capabilities, especially in subregions facing performance challenges. Regional experiences demonstrate that reducing trade costs through measures like digitalization and transport facilitation significantly supports GVC expansion. Policymakers should view the TFA as a baseline standard, encouraging full implementation and striving beyond these minimum requirements. This approach is essential for countries with performance difficulties and for multilateral agencies providing technical assistance and capacity building. Moreover, while many countries have high rates of implementation in various trade facilitation reforms, implementation rates in cross-border paperless trade significantly lag behind.

Looking ahead, it is imperative to adopt digitalization in trade facilitation to enhance GVC resilience and sustainability. The emergence of challenges in GVCs, particularly those highlighted by the COVID-19 pandemic, underscores the need for this role. This calls for accelerating the adoption of the Framework Agreement on Facilitation of Cross-Border Paperless Trade in Asia and the Pacific as well as bilateral and regional digital economy agreements that promote liberalized rules on data flows, electronic transactions, and digital trade facilitation. Continuous support for developing countries is vital in achieving a digitalized trading environment to ensure inclusive, resilient, and sustainable evolution.

Green trade and transport facilitation are crucial to sustainable global trade. Green trade facilitation involves digital measures to reduce carbon emissions, green customs initiatives, and integrating environmental, social, and governance factors into trade finance. Addressing the significant role of international transportation, which accounts for over 10% of trade-related carbon emissions, is essential. The International Transport Forum (2021) predicts a potential doubling of transport activity by 2050, with a corresponding 16% increase in CO_2 emissions, even as freight transport might increase 2.6 times. This expected rise in transport demand highlights the urgent need for stronger decarbonization policies in this sector. Thus, investing in sustainable transport infrastructure is crucial for the eco-friendly movement of goods within GVCs.

Sustainable and resilient global supply chains depend on increased cooperation. Recent trade agreements have made significant strides by incorporating elements of digitalization, but there remains a need to integrate provisions aimed at strengthening supply chains to better withstand various disruptions. The 28th Conference of the Parties (COP28) also underlined the importance of sustainable and resilient supply chains. Key recommended strategies include diversifying supply sources, incorporating advanced technology, and responsible sourcing. Success requires collaboration between governments, the private sector, and stakeholders, supported by access to timely and accurate data for decision-making.

DIGITAL AND SUSTAINABLE TRADE FACILITATION*

---

*   This section is based on the Digital and Sustainable Trade Facilitation in Asia and the Pacific 2023, the regional report by ESCAP on the basis of the United Nations Global Survey on Digital and Sustainable Trade Facilitation. https://www.untfsurvey.org/report.

1 Trade Costs and Trade Facilitation in Asia and the Pacific: State of Play

1.1 | Trade Costs: Subregional Trends

Trade facilitation measures can play a crucial role in mitigating high trade costs by enhancing efficiency through streamlined and digitalized processes. By implementing effective trade facilitation strategies, unnecessary costs can be reduced, helping to counter the trend of increasing trade costs. Yet, trade costs in some subregions of Asia and the Pacific remain high.

Table 1: Intra- and Extra-Regional Comprehensive Trade Costs, 2016–2021 (excluding tariff costs)

Region	ASEAN-4 (%)	East Asia-3 (%)	Russian Federation and Central Asia-3 (%)	Pacific-2 (%)	SAARC-3 (%)	AUS-NZL (%)	EU-3 (%)
ASEAN-4	74.9 (-0.6)	78.6 (3.2)	305.9 (-5.1)	298.8 (8.0)	129.6 (2.9)	104.0 (4.7)	105.3 (-0.2)
East Asia-3	78.6 (3.2)	58.0 (10.0)	167.1 (-0.2)	201.2 (-21.5)	129.3 (5.4)	89.6 (4.4)	85.6 (1.0)
Russian Federation and Central Asia-3	305.9 (-5.1)	167.1 (-0.2)	108.8 (-6.2)	427.5 (29.1)	265.7 (3.8)	310.0 (-13.3)	146.2 (-2.8)
Pacific-2	298.8 (8.0)	201.2 (-21.5)	427.5 (29.1)	89.6 (-19.9)	361.4 (6.8)	102.3 (7.1)	312.1 (0.2)
SAARC-3	129.6 (2.9)	129.3 (5.4)	265.7 (3.8)	361.4 (6.8)	160.7 (37.6)	139.2 (2.3)	117.4 (3.6)
AUS-NZL	104.0 (4.7)	89.6 (4.4)	310.0 (-13.3)	102.3 (7.1)	139.2 (2.3)	52.8 (0.8)	103.0 (-3.5)
EU-3	105.3 (-0.2)	85.6 (1.0)	146.2 (-2.8)	312.1 (0.2)	117.4 (3.6)	103.0 (-3.5)	41.8 (-2.7)
United States	84.4 (-2.1)	66.3 (3.9)	190.7 (8.0)	183.0 (-6.4)	111.7 (-0.2)	97.7 (-1.6)	65.6 (-2.0)

ASEAN = Association of Southeast Asian Nations, AUS = Australia, EU = European Union, NZL = New Zealand, SAARC = South Asian Association for Regional Cooperation.

Notes: Trade costs may be interpreted as tariff equivalents. Percentage changes in trade costs between 2010–2015 and 2016–2021 are in parentheses.

ASEAN-4: Indonesia, Malaysia, the Philippines, Thailand; East Asia-3: the People's Republic of China, Japan, the Republic of Korea; Europe-3: Germany, France, the United Kingdom; SAARC-3: India, Pakistan, Sri Lanka; Pacific -2: Fiji, Samoa; Central Asia-3: Georgia, Kazakhstan, the Kyrgyz Republic.

Source: ESCAP-World Bank Trade Cost Database, accessed 1 July 2023. https://www.unescap.org/resources/escap-world-bank-trade-cost-database.

The United Nations Economic and Social Commission for Asia and the Pacific (ESCAP)–World Bank Trade Cost Database provides a bilateral measure of trade costs, which is comprehensive in the sense that it includes all costs involved in trading goods internationally with another partner (i.e. bilaterally) relative to those involved in trading goods domestically (i.e., intranationally). It captures trade costs in its wider sense, including not only international transport costs and tariffs but also other trade cost components such as direct and indirect costs associated with geographical distance, cultural distance (e.g. language barriers), as well as cumbersome procedures for importing or exporting.[1]

The nontariff trade costs among the three largest European economies (Europe-3) are equivalent to an average of about 42% of the traded goods' value. The intraregional trade costs for the South Asian Association for Regional Cooperation (SAARC-3) amount to a tariff equivalent of 161%. The nontariff trade costs among the Russian Federation and Central Asian countries stand at 109%. In East Asia, the People's Republic of China (PRC), Japan, and the Republic of Korea (East Asia-3), trade costs show a tariff equivalent of 58%, and Association of Southeast Asian Nations (ASEAN) members (ASEAN-4) of 75%. Table 1 presents these figures from the ESCAP–World Bank Trade Cost Database.

Geopolitical conflicts further disrupt global supply chains, and high inflation raise trade costs and uncertainty. While global merchandise trade volumes rebounded strongly after the pandemic, trade growth slowed in 2022 and is expected to remain at a reduced pace throughout 2023, at 0.8%, according to the latest World Trade Organization (WTO) estimate.[2]

1.2 | Implementation of Digital and Sustainable Trade Facilitation Measures

1.2.1 Status of implementation

The regional state of implementation of trade facilitation presented in the chapter is based on the results of the fifth United Nations (UN) Global Survey on Digital and Sustainable Trade Facilitation, conducted in 2023. The UN Global Survey started in 2015 involved all five UN Regional Commissions and gradually expanded to include other international organizations as partners. The UN Global Survey built on earlier efforts from Asia and the Pacific, with the regional surveys on trade facilitation and paperless trade implementation, which took place in 2012 and 2013. These surveys were conducted alongside the Asia-Pacific Trade Facilitation Forums, organized by ESCAP and the Asian Development Bank (ADB). With reliable, comprehensive data on the implementation of conventional and forward-looking trade facilitation measures, regularly surveyed and updated, the UN Global Survey supports evidence-based trade facilitation policies to foster inclusive and sustainable trade.[3]

The 2023 UN Global Survey covers 60 trade facilitation measures, classified into 4 groups and 11 subgroups (Table 2). The first group, *general trade facilitation*, includes many WTO Trade Facilitation Agreement (TFA) measures with subgroups of *transparency, formalities, institutional arrangement and cooperation,* and *transit.* The second group,

---

[1]   Trade cost database is available at (accessed 1 July 2023). https://www.unescap.org/resources/escap-world-bank-trade-cost-database.
[2]   See WTO (2023).
[3]   The survey results are available at https://www.untfsurvey.org.

digital trade facilitation, includes *paperless trade* and *cross-border paperless trade* subgroups, which are related to the UN treaty on trade digitalization (Box 1). The third group, *sustainable trade facilitation*, includes *trade facilitation for SMEs, agricultural trade facilitation,* and *women in trade facilitation* subgroups. The fourth group, *other trade facilitation,* comes with subgroups: *trade finance facilitation* and *trade facilitation in times of crisis*. In addition, *trade facilitation for e-commerce* and *trade facilitation and wildlife protection* measures were added to the survey on a pilot basis.

Table 2: **Grouping of Trade Facilitation Measures and Correspondence with Trade Facilitation Agreement Articles**

Group	Subgroup	Measure	Relevant TFA Article
General Trade Facilitation	Transparency	Publication of existing import–export regulations on the Internet	1.2
		Stakeholders' consultation on new draft regulations (prior to their finalization)	2.2
		Advance publication/notification of new trade-related regulations before their implementation	2.1
		Advance ruling on tariff classification and origin of imported goods	3
		Independent appeal mechanism	4
	Formalities	Risk management	7.4
		Pre-arrival processing	7.1
		Post-clearance audits	7.5
		Separation of release from final determination of customs duties, taxes, fees, and charges	7.3
		Establishment and publication of average release times	7.6
		Trade facilitation measures for authorized operators	7.7
		Expedited shipments	7.8
		Acceptance of copies of original supporting documents required for import, export, or transit formalities	10.2.1
	Institutional arrangement and cooperation	National Trade Facilitation Committee or similar body	23
		National legislative framework and/or institutional arrangements for border agencies cooperation	8
		Government agencies delegating border controls to customs authorities	
		Alignment of working days and hours with neighboring countries at border crossings	8.2(a)
		Alignment of formalities and procedures with neighboring countries at border crossings	8.2(b)
	Transit	Transit facilitation agreement(s)	
		Limit the physical inspections of transit goods	10.5
		Use risk assessment	10.5
		Supporting pre-arrival processing for transit facilitation	11.9

continued next page

Table 2: *Continued*

Group	Subgroup	Measure	Relevant TFA Article
Digital Trade Facilitation	Paperless trade	Automated Customs System	
		Internet connection available to customs and other trade control agencies	
		Electronic single window system	10.4
		Electronic submission of customs declarations	
		Electronic application and issuance of import and export permits	
		Electronic submission of air cargo manifests	
		Electronic application and issuance of preferential certificate of origin	
		E-payment of customs duties and fees	7.2
		Electronic application for Customs Refunds	
	Cross-border paperless trade	Laws and regulations for electronic transactions	
		Recognized certification authority	
		Electronic exchange of customs declaration	
		Electronic exchange of certificate of origin	
		Electronic exchange of sanitary and phytosanitary certificate	
		Paperless collection of payment from a documentary letter of credit	
Sustainable Trade Facilitation	Trade facilitation for SMEs	Trade-related information measures for SMEs	
		SMEs in Authorized Economic Operators scheme	
		SMEs access single window	
		SMEs in the National Trade Facilitation Committee	
		Other special measures for SMEs	
	Agricultural trade facilitation	Testing and laboratory facilities available to meet SPS of main trading partners	7.9
		National standards and accreditation bodies to facilitate compliance with SPS	
		Electronic application and issuance of SPS certificates	
		Special treatment for perishable goods	
	Women in trade facilitation	Trade facilitation policy/strategy to increase women's participation in trade	
		Trade facilitation measures to benefit women involved in trade	
		Women's membership in the National Trade Facilitation Committee or similar bodies	
Other Trade Facilitation	Trade finance facilitation	Single window facilitates traders' access to finance	
		Authorities engaged in blockchain-based supply chain project covering trade finance	
		Variety of trade finance services available	
	Trade facilitation in times of crisis	Agency in place to manage trade facilitation in times of crises and emergencies	
		Online publication of emergency trade facilitation measures	
		Coordination between countries on emergency trade facilitation measures	
		Additional trade facilitation measures to facilitate trade in times of emergencies	
		Plan in place to facilitate trade during future crises	

SMEs = small and medium-sized enterprises, SPS = sanitary and phytosanitary, TFA = trade facilitation agreement.

Source: ESCAP (2024).

Box 1:   Framework Agreement on Facilitation of Cross-Border Paperless Trade in Asia and the Pacific: An Update

The Framework Agreement on Facilitation of Cross-Border Paperless Trade in Asia and the Pacific, a United Nations treaty, aims to foster cross-border paperless trade. It does so by (i) enabling electronic exchange and mutual recognition of trade-related data and documents, and (ii) facilitating interoperability among existing national and subregional single windows and/or other paperless trade systems. The treaty is structured as an inclusive and enabling platform that offers benefits to all participating economies, irrespective of their current standing in trade facilitation or single window/paperless trade implementation.

The treaty, adopted by member states of the Economic and Social Commission for Asia and the Pacific (ESCAP) in 2016, entered into force on 20 February 2021, indicating ESCAP members' continued efforts to accelerate trade digitalization in the region. At the time of publication, 13 countries are parties to the treaty. Azerbaijan acceded in March 2018, followed by the Philippines in December 2019. The Islamic Republic of Iran ratified in May 2020, Bangladesh in October 2020, and the People's Republic of China became the fifth party, ratified in November 2020. Mongolia, the Republic of Korea, Tajikistan, Timor-Leste, Turkmenistan, and Tuvalu acceded in 2022. The Russian Federation and the Kyrgyz Republic acceded in 2023. Armenia and Cambodia signed it in 2017. Several other ESCAP member states are in the process of completing their domestic procedures for joining the treaty.

Several benefits derive from the agreement. First, it enables countries to send a clear signal of high-level commitment and strategic foresight demonstrated by the country's leadership in harnessing the benefits of trade digitalization and actively participating in the rapidly expanding domain of digital trade. Second, with the dedicated institutional framework, parties are supported with increased opportunities for developing legal and technical solutions for trade digitalization. These include pragmatic solutions for exchanging trade documents across borders through pilot projects, capacity-building and technical assistance support, and access to structured and regular sharing of lessons learned on implementation of best practices based on existing international standards. Ultimately, trade digitalization is anticipated to significantly improve efficiency by enabling electronic exchange of trade data and documents, potentially reducing trade costs by approximately 11% in the region and enhancing regulatory compliance.

Source: ESCAP. (n.d.).

The UN Global Survey's scope extends beyond the measures outlined in the WTO TFA. Many paperless trade measures, particularly those related to cross-border paperless trade, are not explicitly covered in the WTO TFA. However, their inclusion in many cases would support better the TFA's implementation in digital form. Similarly, most measures under the *sustainable trade facilitation* group are not explicitly addressed in the WTO TFA, except for some related to *agricultural trade facilitation* measures. The addition of the *other trade facilitation* group considers the role of trade finance in facilitating trade flows, and the challenges posed by crises to the global trade and supply chain.

From January to July of 2023, data for the fifth UN Global Survey were collected. Each of the trade facilitation measures included in the UN Global Survey was rated as either "fully implemented", "partially implemented", "on a pilot basis", "not implemented", or "don't know". A score of 3, 2, 1, or 0 was assigned to each of the four implementation stages to calculate implementation rates for individual measures across countries, subregions, or groupings. Then, the average score for the set of measures was expressed as percentage. For each subgroup, a set of relevant measures was calculated.

Implementation rates of measures under *general* and *digital trade facilitation* subgroups were calculated for 47 countries in Asia and the Pacific (Figure 1). The regional average implementation rate stands at 67%. Implementation of trade facilitation measures varies across the region. Australia, the PRC, India, Japan, the Republic of Korea, New Zealand, and Singapore have average implementation rates above 90%, while those in many Pacific countries barely reach 50%.

Figure 1: Overall Implementation of Trade Facilitation Measures in 47 Asia and Pacific Countries

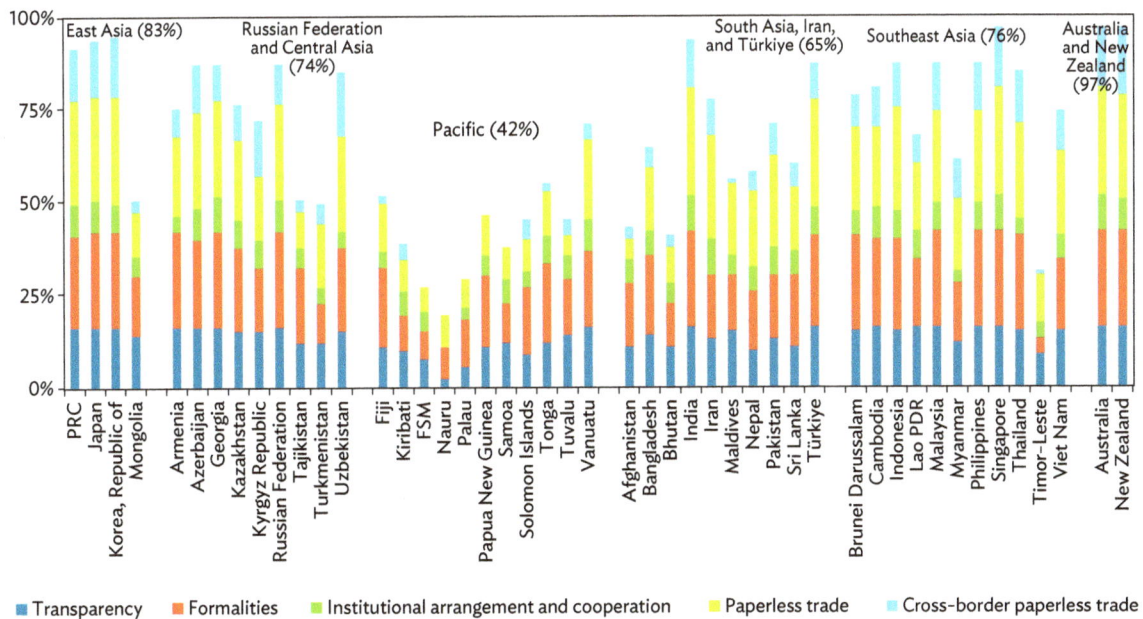

FSM = Federated States of Micronesia, Lao PDR = Lao People's Democratic Republic, PRC = People's Republic of China.

Note: Among the 60 measures surveyed across the United Nations regional commissions, three measures including electronic submission of sea cargo manifests, alignment of working days and hours with neighboring countries at border crossings, and alignment of formalities and procedures with neighboring countries at border crossings are excluded when calculating the overall score as they are not relevant to all countries surveyed. Four transit facilitation measures are also excluded for the same reason. Additionally, sustainable trade facilitation and other trade facilitation are excluded as these newly added groups of measures were not included in the earlier surveys, for comparison.

Source: United Nations (UN). UN Global Survey on Digital and Sustainable Trade Facilitation. 2023 Survey results at untfsurvey.org.

Figure 2 data illustrates implementation rates in six subregions and among three groups of countries with special needs—landlocked developing countries (LLDCs), least developed countries (LDCs), and small island developing states (SIDS). Implementation rates vary significantly among subregions in Asia and the Pacific. Australia and New Zealand exhibited the highest implementation rates at 97%, followed by East Asia at 83%, Southeast Asia 76%, and the Russian Federation and Central Asia 74%.

Figure 2: **Average Trade Facilitation Implementation Rates in Asia and Pacific Subregions and Countries with Special Needs**

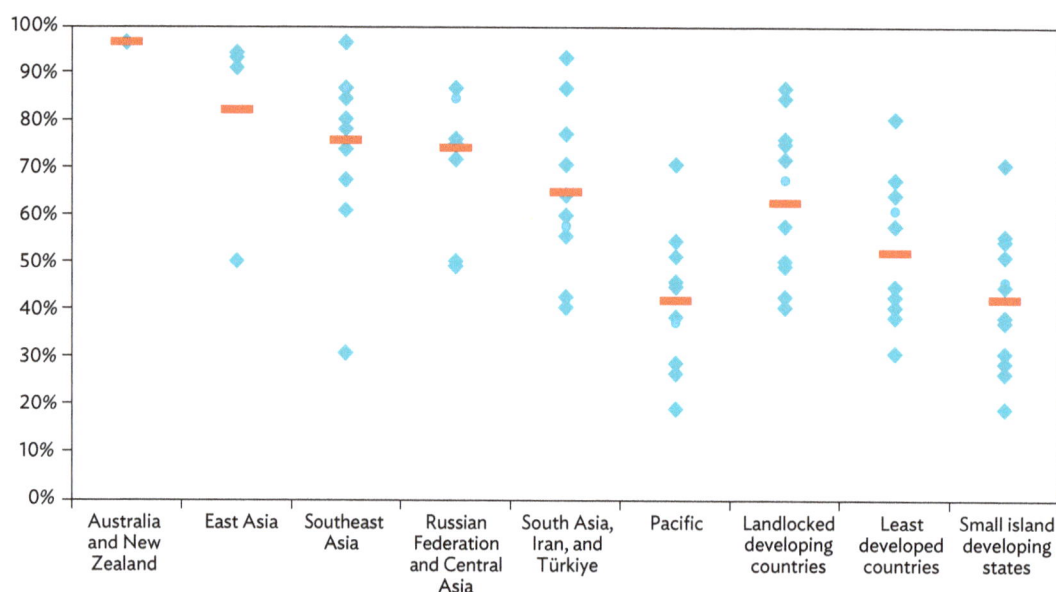

Note: The red bars represent average implementation rates for each group of countries; blue dots show implementation rates for individual economies within each group.

Source: United Nations (UN). UN Global Survey on Digital and Sustainable Trade Facilitation. 2023 Survey results at untfsurvey.org.

On the other hand, some subregions are still catching up, with South Asia, Iran, and Türkiye at 65% and the Pacific at 42%, the two lowest subregional implementation scores. This may be explained by geographical constraints, as many countries in these regions face more significant difficulties in facilitating trade due to factors such as their small size, geographical remoteness, and limited access to maritime trade routes. Adoption of *cross-border paperless trade* also remains low in both regions. Implementing these measures often requires a high level of collaboration between trading partners to be considered "fully implemented". Therefore, the promotion of additional regional and subregional trade agreements and trade facilitation initiatives can drive enhanced cooperation in digital trade.

Figure 2 also shows that the average implementation rates for LDCs, LLDCs, and SIDS are diverse, ranging from 43% to 63%, but all lower than the regional average implementation rate of 67%. Barriers to connectivity, such as poor infrastructure, geographical factors that hinder trade facilitation, or lack of capacity due to multiple factors, put these countries at a disadvantage. LDCs, in particular, are the most vulnerable segment of the international community, with poor infrastructure and limited capacity and resources. LLDCs have no direct sea access, making trade logistics more complex and expensive. In SIDS, high communication and logistics costs can hamper ability to participate in international trade. The international community therefore needs to support LDCs, LLDCs, and SIDS efforts to improve trade facilitation by addressing specific needs and providing technical assistance and capacity-building support.

Nevertheless, LLDCs have demonstrated higher average levels of trade facilitation compared to LDCs or SIDS, which can be attributed to the coordinated support provided to address the specific requirements of LLDCs. For example, the Vienna Programme of Action for Landlocked Developing Countries 2014–2024 prioritizes the unique development challenges faced by landlocked nations. It strongly emphasizes international trade and trade facilitation, focusing on building efficient transit systems, developing transport infrastructure, enhancing competitiveness, expanding trade, structural transformation, and regional cooperation, among other measures to transform these landlocked countries into well-connected and land-linked nations (United Nations 2024). Moreover, the majority of landlocked developing countries in Asia and the Pacific are members of the Central Asia Regional Economic Cooperation (CAREC). These countries are carrying out the CAREC Integrated Trade Agenda 2030 and Rolling Strategic Action Plan 2021-2023, which aims to offer a more cohesive strategy for trade policy and trade facilitation matters, as well as provide technical support to facilitate ongoing customs reforms and improve the movement of goods within the CAREC region.[4]

According to Figure 3 and Table 3, all countries in the region are engaged in significant but varying degrees in implementing *general trade facilitation*. The *transparency* sub-group stands out with the highest implementation level, at 83%. Within this sub-group, the *publication of import-export regulations on the internet* measure takes the lead, with 98% of the countries having it implemented, at least on a pilot basis. Full implementation has been achieved in 68% of the countries.

Figure 3: **Implementation of Subgroups of Trade Facilitation Measures, Asia and Pacific Regional Average**

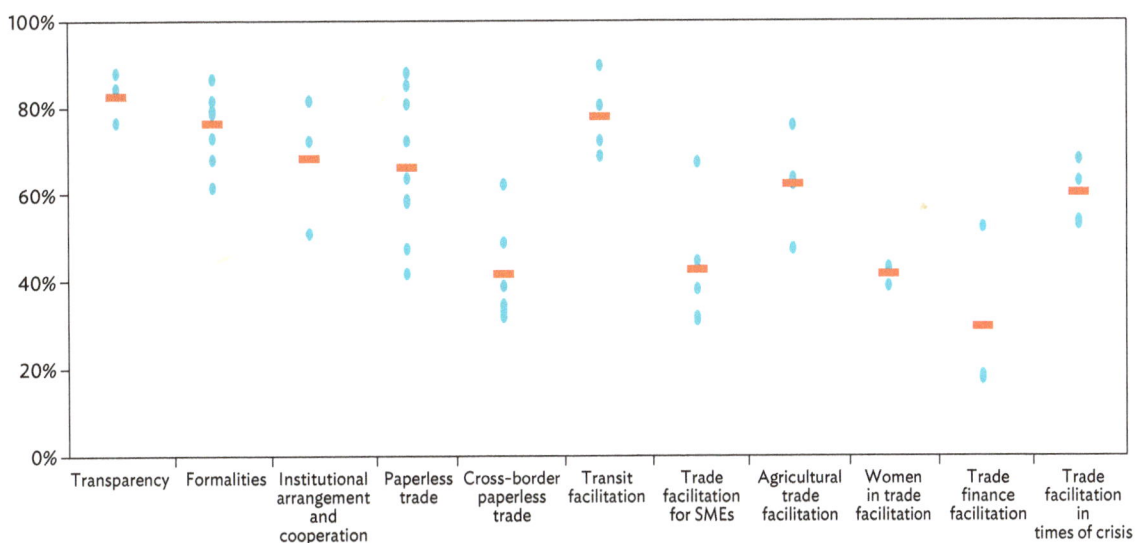

SMEs = small and medium-sized enterprises.

Note: The red bars represent average implementation rates for each group of countries; blue dots show implementation rates for individual economies within each group.

Source: United Nations (UN). UN Global Survey on Digital and Sustainable Trade Facilitation. 2023 Survey results at untfsurvey.org.

4   CAREC Program. CITA Rolling Strategic Action Plan 2021-2023. Appendix 2. carecprogram.org.

Table 3: **Most and Least Implemented Measures in Asia and the Pacific**

Category	Most Implemented (% of countries)		Least Implemented (% of countries)	
	Measure	Implemented fully, partially and on a pilot basis (%)/Full implementation (%)	Measure	Implemented fully, partially and on a pilot basis (%) / Full implementation (%)
Transparency	Publication of existing import–export regulations on the internet	97.9/68.1	Independent appeal mechanism and online lodging	91.5/51.1
Formalities	Acceptance of copies of original supporting documents required for import, export, or transit formalities	95.7/70.2	TF measures for authorized operators	85.1/34.0
Institutional arrangement and cooperation	National Trade Facilitation Committee or similar body	95.7/59.6	Government agencies delegating border controls to customs authorities	70.2/23.4
Paperless trade	Automated Customs System	100.0/66.0	Electronic application for customs refunds	51.1/27.7
Cross-border paperless trade	Laws and regulations for electronic transactions	89.4/25.5	Paperless collection of payment from a documentary letter of credit	48.9/14.9
Transit facilitation	Limit the physical inspections of transit goods and use risk assessment	61.7/42.6	Supporting pre-arrival processing for transit facilitation	59.6/25.5
Trade facilitation for SMEs	Trade-related information measures for SMEs	85.1/38.3	SMEs access single window	46.8/12.8
Agricultural trade facilitation	Special treatment for perishable goods	91.5/48.9	Electronic application and issuance of SPS certificates	72.3/19.1
Women in trade facilitation	TF measures to benefit women involved in trade	72.3/14.9	TF policy/strategy to increase women's participation in trade	55.3/14.9
Trade finance facilitation	Variety of trade finance services available	76.6/17.0	Authorities engaged in blockchain-based supply chain project covering trade finance	29.8/2.1
Trade facilitation in times of crisis	Online publication of emergency TF measures	89.4/42.6	Plan in place to facilitate trade during future crises	72.3/23.4

SMEs = small and medium-sized enterprises, SPS = sanitary and phytosanitary, TF = trade facilitation.

Source: United Nations (UN). UN Global Survey on Digital and Sustainable Trade Facilitation. 2023 Survey results at untfsurvey.org.

Following these, *transit and formalities* subgroups have the second and third highest implementation rates, at 76% and 78%, respectively. In the *formalities* subgroup, the most widely implemented measure is *acceptance of copies of original documents required for import, export, or transit formalities* (96% of countries surveyed), while in the *transit* subgroup, *limit the physical inspections of transit goods and use risk assessment* that has been most widely implemented, with 62% of countries surveyed having implemented it.

The *institutional arrangements and cooperation* subgroup shows an average implementation rate of 68% among the countries surveyed. The measure related to the creation of a *national trade facilitation committee or similar body* has been implemented by 96% of countries, reflecting the strong commitment of Asia and Pacific countries to improving trade processes and cooperation at the institutional level. In contrast, the measure with the lowest implementation rate, *government agencies delegating border controls to customs authorities*, has been adopted by 70% of countries, with only 23% achieving full implementation. This indicates a need for increased cooperation and coordination between government agencies and customs authorities.

In the *digital trade facilitation* group, the implementation level of the *paperless trade* subgroup is 66%. Nonetheless, the rates of implementation vary significantly based on the measure being considered. For example, all countries have implemented, at least on a pilot basis, *automated customs systems*. In contrast, the measure, with the lowest implementation rate, *electronic application for customs refunds*, has only been adopted by 51% of the surveyed countries. On the other hand, the implementation level of the *cross-border paperless trade* subgroup is significantly lower at 42%. Most countries have implemented the measure *laws and regulations for electronic transactions* (89%), and 26% of countries have fully implemented this measure, making it the most implemented in this subgroup. The disparity between the most and least implemented measures is quite significant, as the measure *paperless collection of payment from a documentary letter of credit* has been implemented by 49% of countries, and only 15% achieved full implementation, making it the least implemented of this subgroup. This highlights the need for closer intergovernmental cooperation on cross-border paperless trade to build greater interoperability between national systems. Noting the important role that *digital trade facilitation* plays, a new metric has been developed for assessing global progress in digitalizing trade procedures (Box 2).

Among the *sustainable trade facilitation* group, *agricultural trade facilitation* measures have been relatively well implemented, with an average of 62% implementation. As Table 3 indicates, the measure *special treatment for perishable goods* is the most implemented in this subgroup, with 49% of the countries surveyed having fully implemented it. Nevertheless, when it comes to *the electronic application and issuance of sanitary and phytosanitary (SPS) certificates*, this percentage drops to 19%, making it the least implemented measure of this subgroup. On the other hand, implementation of measures to improve opportunities for SMEs remains low, at 43%. Specifically, the measure *SMEs access to single window* has been fully implemented by only 13% of the countries. Similarly, the implementation rate of measures related to *women in trade facilitation* stands at 42%. For *TF measures to benefit women involved in trade*, which is the most implemented measure in this subgroup, only 15% of the countries have fully implemented them. This indicates that the presence of policies and initiatives addressing inclusiveness in trade facilitation is still insufficient in Asia and the Pacific.

Digital trade transformation can contribute to sustainable development objectives by reducing obstacles. Figure 4 shows the strong positive correlation between the digital and sustainable aspects of trade facilitation. Countries with higher implementation rates for digital trade facilitation measures have also demonstrated commendable performance in sustainable trade facilitation measures. Generally, more advanced countries have excelled in both the digital and sustainable dimensions compared to their less advanced counterparts. The Republic of Korea leads in sustainable trade facilitation, with a 100% implementation rate, followed by the PRC, at 96%. Meanwhile, New Zealand leads in digital trade facilitation, with an implementation rate of 96%. Following closely are Australia, the Republic of Korea, and Singapore, all achieving a 93% implementation rate.

**Box 2: Trade Digitalization Index: A Novel Measure Assessing
         Global Progress in Digitalizing Trade Procedures**

The Trade Digitalization Index (TDI) is a new metric designed to assess the global progress in digitalizing trade procedures. It is based on data from the UN Global Survey on Digital and Sustainable Trade Facilitation. The TDI, accounts for the implementation of two key subgroups of measures in the survey, *paperless trade* and *cross-border paperless trade*.

The figure below illustrates the rates of trade digitalization across different regions. It is noteworthy that there is a 53 percentage-point difference in implementation rates among the different regions, with significant disparities also evident within regions. Generally, advanced economies outperform developing ones in trade digitalization. The wide gaps in implementation highlight the urgent need for collaborative efforts on a global and regional scale to achieve effective trade digitalization. They may be addressed through dedicated intergovernmental agreements emphasizing capacity building and pilot projects, such as the Framework Agreement on Facilitation of Cross-Border Paperless Trade in Asia and the Pacific (Box 1).

Average Trade Digitalization Rates Around the World, 2023

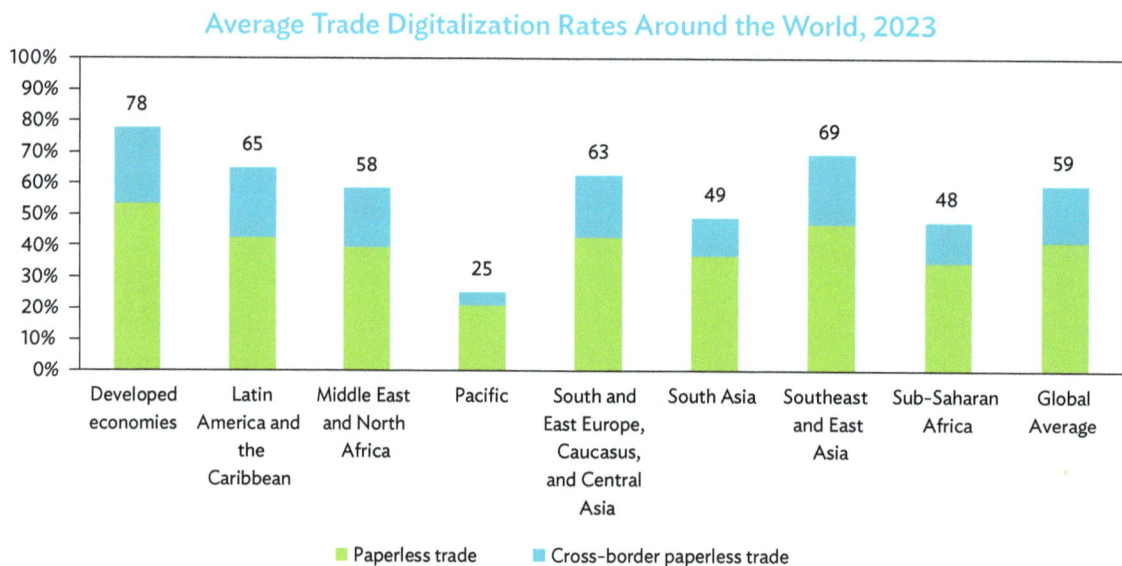

Source: Duval, Prince, and Utoktham (2024).

The average implementation rate of *trade finance facilitation* measures is relatively low, standing at 30%. Not only is the measure *authorities engaged in blockchain-based supply chain project covering trade finance* the lowest measure implemented in this subgroup, but it is also the least implemented measure in the entire survey, with only about 2% of the countries surveyed having fully implemented it. On the other hand, countries in Asia and the Pacific have implemented the *variety of trade finance services available* measure relatively well, with nearly 77% of the countries surveyed having implemented it, at least on a pilot basis.

Finally, the average implementation rate of the *trade facilitation in times of crisis* measure stands at 60%, responding to the recent disruptions in global trade due to various crises. In this context, countries surveyed focused particularly on the *online publication of emergency TF measures*, the most implemented in this subgroup. In addition, the percentage of countries adopting long-term resilience measures is significant, with 72% implementing a *plan in place to facilitate trade during future crises*, at least on a pilot basis. Nevertheless, room remains for improvement, as only 23% of the countries have fully implemented this measure, making it the least implemented in this subgroup.

Figure 4: **Implementation of Digital and Sustainable Dimensions of Trade Facilitation**

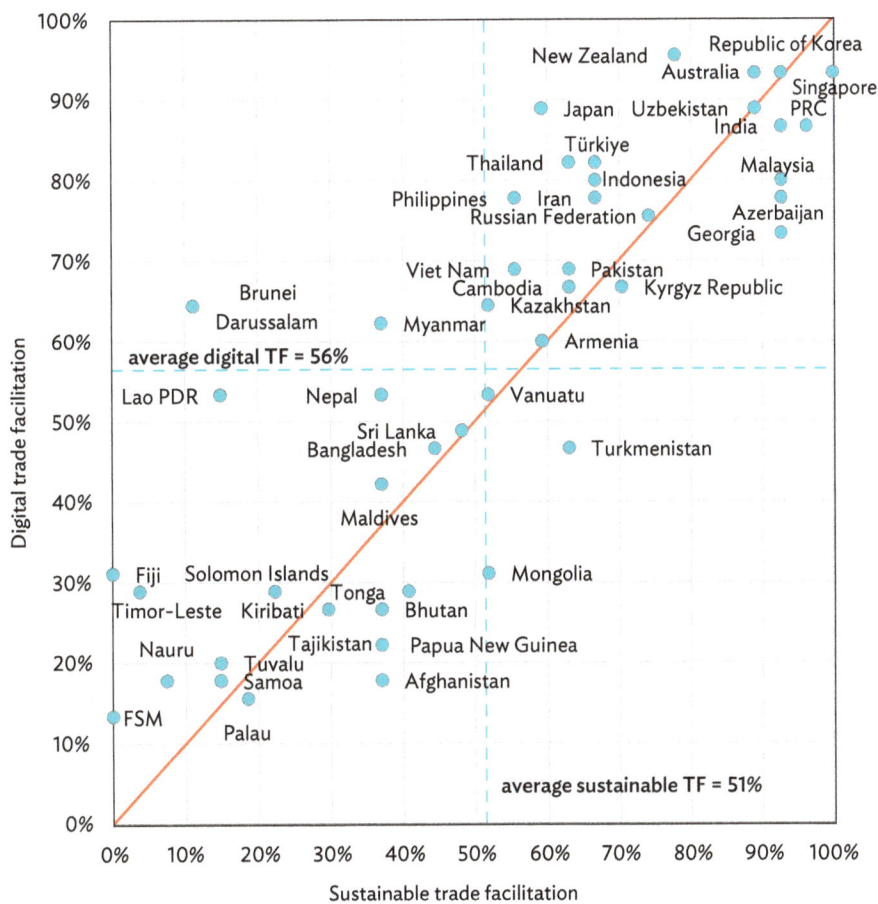

FSM = Federated States of Micronesia, Lao PDR = Lao People's Democratic Republic, PRC = People's Republic of China, TF = trade facilitation.

Source: United Nations (UN). UN Global Survey on Digital and Sustainable Trade Facilitation. 2023 Survey results at untfsurvey.org.

1.2.2 Progress in implementation from 2019 to 2023

Figure 5 shows trade facilitation progress based on subregional implementation rates from 2019 to 2023 across three UN Global Survey results. A significant increase of 6 percentage points from 2019 to 2021 was noted in Asia and the Pacific, partially driven by the swift adoption of digital trade facilitation measures as a response to the COVID-19 pandemic. Building on progress, countries continued to enhance efficiency through streamlined and digitalized trade processes and recorded a moderate increase of 3 percentage points in 2023 over 2021, reaching 67%.

Figure 5: **Trade Facilitation Implementation by Subregions in Asia and the Pacific, 2019, 2021, and 2023**

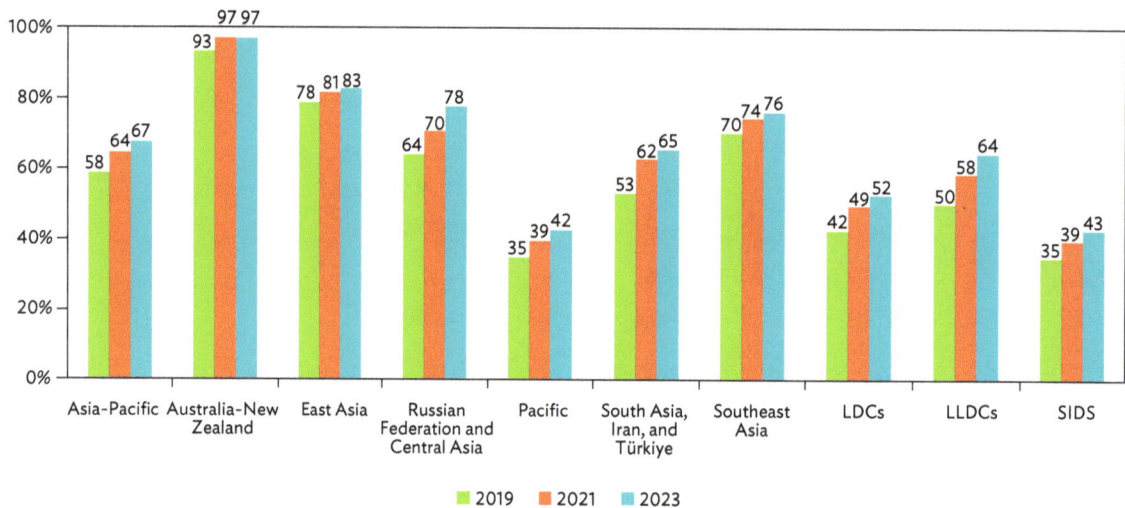

LDCs = least developed countries, LLDCs = landlocked developing countries, SIDS = small island developing states.

Note: Figure 5 is based on 31 general trade facilitation measures of 46 common countries.

Source: United Nations (UN). UN Global Survey on Digital and Sustainable Trade Facilitation. 2023 Survey results at untfsurvey.org.

This upward trend is encouraging, and all subregions have experienced an increase in their trade facilitation measures implementation rate from 2019 to 2023. Specifically, the highest progress has been observed in the Russian Federation and Central Asia, with an increase in the implementation rate of 6 percentage points from 2019 to 2021 and 8 percentage points from 2021 to 2023. Similarly, significant progress has been observed in LLDCs, where the implementation rate increased by 8 percentage points from 2019 to 2021 and 6 percentage points from 2021 to 2023. This progress is particularly impressive, as LLDCs face additional challenges due to no direct sea access, making trade logistics more complex and expensive.

Figure 6 shows that commendable progress was made from 2019 to 2023, across three UN Global Survey results, in implementing specific measures related to *digital trade facilitation* with the *paperless trade* and *cross-border paperless trade* subgroups. Implementation rates for *paperless trade* rose by 6 percentage points from 2019 to 2021 and 4 percentage points from 2021 to 2023. Implementation rates for *cross-border paperless trade* increased 7 percentage points and 4 percentage points for the same period. As mentioned, the acceleration of *digital trade facilitation* measures was prominent from 2019 to 2021 in response to the COVID-19 crisis. Still, countries continued improving in this area from 2021 and 2023, although more moderate progress is observed. However, *digital trade facilitation* implementation rates are still not as high as those recorded for *general trade facilitation* measures. This highlights the need to continue the progress made by continuous efforts to develop paperless trade systems and better coordinate to ensure interoperability between countries.

Figure 6: **Average Implementation of Different Subgroups of Trade Facilitation Measures in Asia and the Pacific, 2019, 2021, and 2023**

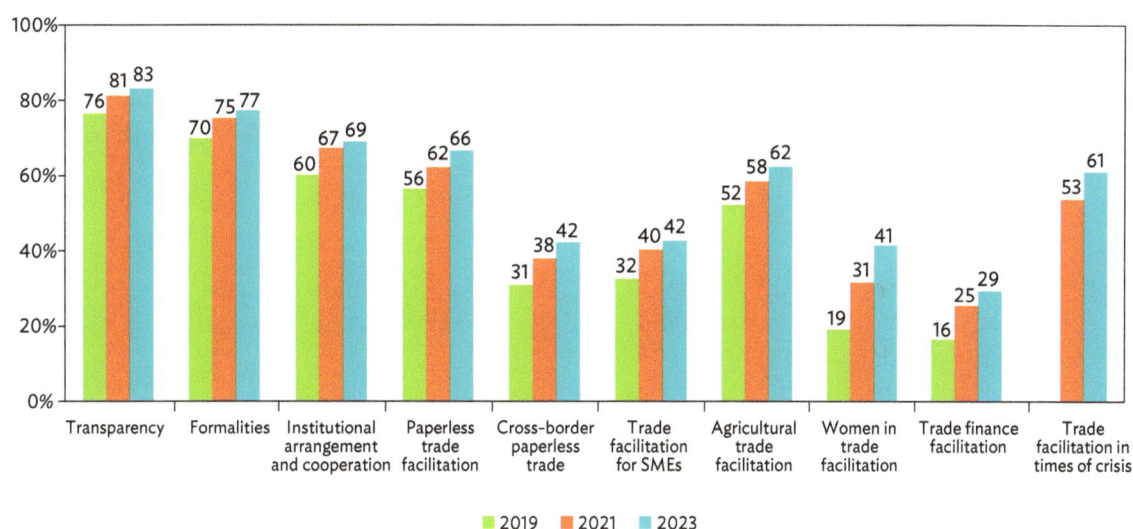

SMEs = small and medium-sized enterprises.

Note: The comparison for 2019–2023 is based on 46 countries, including trade facilitation in times of crisis (only available for 2021 and 2023).

Source: United Nations (UN). UN Global Survey on Digital and Sustainable Trade Facilitation. 2023 Survey results at untfsurvey.org.

2 Impact of Trade Facilitation on Trade

To quantify trade facilitation's impact on regional trade flows, this section presents a gravity model to examine trade flow changes resulting from improved trade facilitation and trade infrastructure, such as port connectivity. The section also explores the impact of trade facilitation on trade costs to economies, as discussed in United Nations (2023), and counterfactual simulations based on trade cost models, as in ESCAP (n.d.).

2.1 | Gravity Model of Trade and Data

Policies and trade cost factors from Arvis et al. (2016) are incorporated into the gravity model to examine their effects and trade flows. These include geographical factors (distance, adjacency of countries, and "landlockedness"), cultural distance (common official/unofficial language, colonial relationships, having a common colonizer, and previously identical country), existence of trade policies (regional trade agreements or tariffs), prevalence of infrastructure (liner shipping connectivity index [LSCI]) for trade. In addition, trade facilitation implementation is also included as a factor expected to affect trade flows. Accordingly, the extended specification of the gravity model of trade is as follows:

$$
\begin{aligned}
\ln(x_{ij}) = {} & \beta_0 + \beta_1 \ln(gdp_i) + \beta_2 \ln(gdp_j) + \beta_3 \ln(gtariff_{ij}) + \beta_4 \ln(dist_{ij}) + \beta_5(contig_{ij}) \\
& + \beta_6(comlang\_off_{ij}) + \beta_7(comlang\_ethno_{ij}) + \beta_8(colony_{ij}) + \beta_9(comcol_{ij}) + \beta_{10}(smctry_{ij}) \\
& + \beta_{11}(rta_{ij}) + \beta_{12}(landlocked_{ij}) + \beta_{13} \ln(LSCI_i) + \beta_{14} \ln(TF_i) + D_j + \varepsilon_{ij}
\end{aligned}
$$

Table 4 summarizes variables, treatment of data (when applicable), source of data, and predicted expected effects on trade cost factors. Trade facilitation implementation is computed based on 31 general and digital trade facilitation measures in the 2023 UN Global Survey.[5] The model also includes partner fixed effect (Dj) and robust and clustered standard errors by country pair to take care of cross-country heterogeneity. The model is estimated across a cross-section of 111 reporting countries using ordinary least squares.

---

[5] Survey data for 2021 were updated based on the data collected in 2023. This is to ensure it corresponds with the latest data from the ESCAP-World Bank trade cost database in 2019–2021.

Table 4: Data Source, Definition, Treatment, Source, and Expected Sign

Variable	Definition	Data Treatment	Source	Expected Sign
x_{ij}	Exports of goods	Average of 2019–2021	World Integrated Trade Solutions (WITS) Database	
gdp_i/gdp_j	Gross domestic product of reporting country (i)/ trade partner (j)	Average of 2019–2021	World Development Indicators (WDI), World Bank	+
$gtariff_{ij}$	Geometric average tariff (1+rate) that each reporter (i) charges to its partner (j) and vice versa. Formula is as follows: $$gtariff_{ijt} = \sqrt{tariff_{ijt} \times tariff_{ijt}}$$	Average of 2019–2021	WITS Database	–
$dist_{ij}$	Geographical distance between country i and j.	…	CEPII	–
$contig_{ij}$	Dummy variable of contiguity equal to 1 if country i and j share a common border and zero otherwise.	…	CEPII	+
$comlang\_off_{ij}$	Dummy variable of common official language equal to 1 if country i and j use the same common official language and 0 otherwise.	…	CEPII	+
$comlang\_ethno_{ij}$	Dummy variable of common language equal to 1 if a language is spoken by at least 9% of the population in both countries and zero otherwise.	…	CEPII	+
$colony_{ij}$	Dummy variable equal to 1 if country i and j were ever in colonial relationship and zero otherwise.	…	CEPII	+
$comcol_{ij}$	Dummy variable equal to 1 if country i and j had a common colonizer after 1945 and zero otherwise.	…	CEPII	+
$smctry_{ij}$	Dummy variable equal to 1 if country i and j were or are the same country and zero otherwise.	…	CEPII	+
rta_{ij}	Dummy variable equal to 1 if country i and j are members of the same regional trade agreement and zero otherwise.	Latest definition in 2021	Egger, P. H. and Larch, M. (2008)	+
$landlocked_{ij}$	Dummy variable equal to 1 if either country i or j is landlocked and zero otherwise.	…	CEPII	–
$LSCI_i$	Average scores of liner shipping connectivity index of country i.	Data gaps filled/average 2019–2021	UNCTAD	+
TF_i	TF implementation (in percent) of country i, modelled as: (a) overall TF (tfi_i); or (b) general TF (generaltf_i) + digital TF (pxbptf_i).	0.0001 replacement if value is zero/ survey data 2021 with 2019 replacement if data are not available	UN Global Survey on Trade Facilitation and Paperless Trade Implementation: 2023	+

… = not applicable, CEPII = Le Centre d'Études Prospectives et d'Informations Internationales, ESCAP = Economic and Social Commission for Asia and the Pacific, UNCTAD = United Nations Conference on Trade and Development.

Note: Where available, the average of the latest data from 2019 onward is applied in the models. The percentage of trade facilitation implementation of 2021 is used as trade flows data of 2023 is incomplete. The study assumes that implementation is at the level of 2019 if those economies do not submit data for 2021. Data filling for liner shipping connectivity is required to ensure inclusion of landlocked economies. Port countries are used as proxies for landlocked countries' portal performance. For the trade facilitation components, zeros are substituted by 0.0001 to prevent exclusion of observations from the estimation.

Source: Authors.

2.2 | Empirical Results

Table 5 shows results of estimates from the gravity model. The model is distinguished into two main trade facilitation specifications: model (1) estimates overall trade facilitation implementation based on 31 main trade facilitation measures; and model (2) segregates effects into two groups of trade facilitation measures defined in Table 4—general trade facilitation (transparency, formality, and institutional arrangement and cooperation measures) and digital trade facilitation (paperless and cross-border paperless trade measures).

The impacts on trade flows of tariffs, regional trade agreements, trade-related infrastructure (liner shipping connectivity), as well as trade facilitation implementation, are all statistically significant and as expected. Table 5 shows that trade liberalization remains important despite the significant tariff cuts achieved over the past 2 decades. A 1% reduction in tariff leads to an increase in trade flows of nearly 2%. In comparison, the model suggests that incremental improvements in hard trade-related infrastructure yield less than a 0.1% increase in trade, on average.

Table 5: **Gravity Model of Trade Results**

	Beta Coefficient		Standardized Beta	
Dependent Variable: ln_x_{ij}	(1) Overall TFI	(2) General TFI + Paperless TFI	(3) Overall TFI	(4) General TFI + Paperless TFI
ln_gdpi	1.225*** [84.61]	1.240*** [87.02]	0.593*** [84.61]	0.601*** [87.02]
ln_gdpj	0.883*** [21.56]	0.882*** [21.29]	0.492*** [21.56]	0.492*** [21.29]
ln_tariff	-1.946*** [-4.467]	-1.948*** [-4.466]	-0.0278*** [-4.467]	-0.0278*** [-4.466]
ln_dist	-1.458*** [-53.84]	-1.459*** [-53.91]	-0.299*** [-53.84]	-0.300*** [-53.91]
contig	0.563*** [4.630]	0.563*** [4.645]	0.0216*** [4.630]	0.0216*** [4.645]
comlang_off	0.165* [1.938]	0.213** [2.468]	0.0143* [1.938]	0.0185** [2.468]
comlang_ethno	0.187** [2.237]	0.137 [1.615]	0.0163** [2.237]	0.0119 [1.615]
colony	0.589*** [5.388]	0.583*** [5.351]	0.0200*** [5.388]	0.0198*** [5.351]
comcol	0.866*** [11.22]	0.855*** [11.07]	0.0604*** [11.22]	0.0596*** [11.07]
smctry	0.668*** [3.352]	0.621*** [3.122]	0.0167*** [3.352]	0.0155*** [3.122]
landlocked_ij	-0.888*** [-15.49]	-0.825*** [-14.15]	-0.106*** [-15.49]	-0.0985*** [-14.15]

continued next page

Table 5: *Continued*

Dependent Variable: ln_x$_{ij}$	Beta Coefficient		Standardized Beta	
	(1) Overall TFI	(2) General TFI + Paperless TFI	(3) Overall TFI	(4) General TFI + Paperless TFI
rta	0.625*** [13.95]	0.626*** [13.99]	0.0756*** [13.95]	0.0758*** [13.99]
ln_lsci_i	0.0443* [1.776]	0.0339 [1.363]	0.0105* [1.776]	0.00805 [1.363]
ln_tfi_i	1.513*** [17.91]		0.110*** [17.91]	
ln_generaltf_i		0.517*** [5.175]		0.0347*** [5.175]
ln_pxbptf_i		0.712*** [12.74]		0.0831*** [12.74]
Constant	-30.98*** [-23.68]	-29.16*** [-22.11]		
Observations	15,077	15,077	15,077	15,077
R-squared	0.739	0.739	0.739	0.739
Reporter FE	No	No	No	No
Partner FE	Yes	Yes	Yes	Yes
Adjusted R-squared	0.736	0.736	0.736	0.736

FE = fixed effects, TFI = trade facilitation indicator

Note: Regression estimates of Equation [1] use data specified in Table 4.

*** p<0.01, ** p<0.05, and * p<0.1; t-stats in square parentheses.

Source: Authors' calculations.

The results also confirm the importance of streamlining trade procedures: a 1% improvement in overall trade facilitation implementation results in a more than 1.5% increase in trade, on average. The standardized beta coefficients shown in Table 5 further indicate that trade facilitation reform has a greater potential than trade liberalization (tariff reduction) in enhancing trade flows.[6] The estimates from the model (2) also suggest that trade digitalization should be prioritized in upcoming trade facilitation reforms. Indeed, the impact of a 1% improvement in digital trade facilitation on trade is an average increase of approximately 0.7%. In contrast, the impact of a similar improvement in already well-implemented general trade facilitation measures is only 0.5%.

---

[6] The standardized beta coefficients suggest that improvement in overall trade facilitation implementation by 1 standard deviation (SD) leads to 0.1 SD increase in trade, while 1 SD reduction in tariff improves trade by only 0.02 SD.

2.3 | Impact of Trade Facilitation on Trade Costs

While the empirical results confirmed significant impact on trade flows from trade facilitation implementation, this is typically achieved through reduction in trade costs. The United Nations (2023) assessed trade facilitation impact on trade costs, finding that trade policies (tariffs and regional trade agreements), trade-related infrastructure (e.g., LSCI), and trade facilitation are all statistically significant and have the expected impact on trade costs. However, further questions arise about what the magnitude of trade cost reduction will be when a country improves a set of trade facilitation measures.

Therefore, based on the results of ESCAP (n.d.), this study conducts counterfactual simulations to identify the potential effects of three "cases" of trade facilitation reforms in trade cost reduction across countries as follows:[7]

- Case 1: Binding measures under the World Trade Organization (WTO) Trade Facilitation Agreement (TFA) implemented

- Case 2: Binding and nonbinding measures under the WTO TFA implemented

- Case 3: Binding and nonbinding measures under the WTO TFA, together with digital trade facilitation measures not integrated in the WTO TFA (WTO TFA+), implemented

The following two scenarios are considered for each case:

- Scenario 1: Partially implemented trade facilitation measures in each case. All countries whose trade facilitation measures are either not implemented or are implemented on a pilot basis take action to achieve at least partial implementation.

- Scenario 2: Fully implemented trade facilitation measures in each case. All countries whose trade facilitation measures have not achieved full implementation take action to achieve full implementation.

Table 6 shows simulation results for economies in Asia and the Pacific.[8] Partially implementing only binding measures results in less than a 1% trade cost reduction, while full implementation of only binding measures gives at best a 3% reduction in trade costs. A more ambitious result from full implementation of both binding and nonbinding measures shows at least a 5% decrease in trade costs. Under a WTO TFA+ case where digital trade facilitation measures are implemented additionally, the average trade cost reduction across countries increases to approximately 11% in case of full implementation.

Table 6 also illustrates the average reduction of trade costs in Asia and the Pacific associated with two different groups of trade facilitation measures, i.e., general trade facilitation measures and digital trade facilitation measures. Both scenarios of partial and full implementation indicate that the largest trade cost reduction is from partial or full implementation of paperless and cross-border paperless trade measures, which goes beyond what is required in the WTO TFA.

---

[7]   See Annex 1 Table 1.3 in Duval, Utoktham, and Kravchenko (2018) for the nature and relationships between selected trade facilitation measures considered and the WTO TFA provisions.

[8]   See ESCAP (2024) for the impact on trade cost reduction at a country and subregional level.

Country data show that a reduction in trade costs from their WTO TFA implementation in many developing countries, especially ASEAN and East Asian countries, may be limited. This is because these countries have already implemented many binding and/or nonbinding measures under the WTO TFA, as indicated in their notifications to the WTO, even before the agreement was concluded in 2013. Also, some of these ASEAN and East Asian countries have accomplished certain measures of advanced WTO TFA/WTO TFA+ measures.

In advancing their efforts, countries should pursue digitalization of trade procedures and enable seamless electronic exchange of data and documents across countries. Such endeavors may include initiatives like enhancing interoperability among single windows across countries and regions, harnessing emerging technologies, implementing e-certificates for sanitary and phytosanitary purposes, enhancing e-commerce laws for cross-border, developing cross-border mobile applications, among other relevant measures.

Table 6: Changes in International Trade Costs of Asia and the Pacific as a Result of Alternative Trade Facilitation Reforms

Asia-Pacific: Trade Costs Model	WTO TFA (binding only)		WTO TFA (binding + nonbinding)		WTO TFA+ (binding + nonbinding + other paperless and cross-border paperless trade)	
	Partially Implemented	Fully Implemented	Partially Implemented	Fully Implemented	Partially Implemented	Fully Implemented
Model 1						
Overall trade facilitation	-0.59%	-2.68%	-1.15%	-4.61%	-5.15%	-11.05%
Model 2						
General trade facilitation measures	-0.46%	-2.05%	-0.61%	-2.94%	-0.86%	-3.42%
Digital trade facilitation measures	–	–	-0.50%	-1.12%	-4.10%	-6.95%

– = no measures, WTO TFA = World Trade Organization Trade Facilitation Agreement.
Note: There are no digital trade facilitation measures classified as binding measures under the WTO.
Source: Authors' calculations.

It is also worth identifying magnitudes of trade cost reductions associated with trade-related infrastructural reforms at large, which may incorporate improvements in transport and other trade-related infrastructure and services.[9] Thus, the following additional simulation scenario was conducted using regression estimates:

• Scenario 3: Enhancement in maritime connectivity. Countries with liner shipping connectivity scores below the developing country average/high income (Organisation for Economic Co-operation and Development) average take action to bring their scores to equivalent levels.

---

[9]   See WTO World Trade Report 2015 for a comprehensive discussion on definitions of trade facilitation (WTO 2015).

Table 7: Changes in Trade Costs of Asia and the Pacific from Better Port Connectivity

	Improve to Developing Economies' Average (model 1/model 2)	Improve to OECD Average (model 1/model 2)
Maritime connectivity	-2.14%/-2.17%	-4.37%/-4.44%

OECD = Organisation for Economic Co-operation and Development.
Source: Authors' calculation.

As shown in Table 7, improvement of maritime connectivity, as in scenario 3, would reduce trade costs in Asia and the Pacific by 2% to 4%, on average. However, country-level analysis shows that trade cost reductions from improving maritime connectivity for countries with below-average connectivity are significantly larger than those these countries could achieve by implementing WTO TFA. Taken together, the results point to the need for balance and coordination in the implementation of hard and soft infrastructure improvements.

3 Conclusion and Way Forward

The regional analysis of data from the 2023 UN Global Survey on Digital and Sustainable Trade Facilitation shows that the regional average implementation rate for 31 *general* and *digital trade facilitation* measures stands at 67% in 2023. Based on 46 common countries, an increase of 3 percentage points was observed in 2023 compared with 2021. Despite a moderate increase compared to the 6-percentage points progress observed from 2019 to 2021, it reflects ongoing efforts by countries in the region to enhance efficiency through streamlined and digitalized trade processes. Particular noteworthy progress is observed in the Russian Federation and Central Asia and landlocked developing countries (LLDCs) despite significant challenges and disruptions in the supply chain.

The majority of countries have effectively implemented the *general trade facilitation* group of measures, which aim to improve transparency, reduce unnecessary formalities, and build institutional frameworks for trade facilitation. In addition, countries have continued their progress in digitalization of their trade procedures. These include initiatives such as building and enhancing their national paperless systems, including electronic single window, and implementing integrated and compatible platforms bilaterally and subregionally to support cross-border electronic data exchange, including accelerating data exchange through the ASEAN Single Window. Still, there remains considerable variation in the implementation of *paperless trade* measures, suggesting the potential for further advancement in this area.

However, the implementation of cross-border paperless trade has remained low at 42%, as many developing economies within the region are still in the nascent phases of constructing their national paperless systems. Simultaneously, whereas more advanced economies have successfully instituted paperless systems, yet these systems need comprehensive interoperability.

Based on the most recent data, the analysis reaffirms the significant advantages that digital trade facilitation measures can bring to countries in the region. Empirical evidence indicates that full implementation of digital trade facilitation measures, surpassing the commitments outlined in the WTO TFA, could lead to an approximately 11% reduction in average trade costs in the region. This reduction is 6 percentage points more than the expected reduction from compliance with the WTO TFA binding and nonbinding requirements.

Looking ahead, the implementation of trade facilitation measures should be seen as a gradual process, focusing on specific groups of measures outlined in the UN Global Survey (Figure 7). This process begins with establishing the necessary institutional arrangements to prioritize and coordinate trade facilitation efforts. Subsequently, transparency is enhanced sharing information on laws, regulations, and procedures and involving stakeholders in their development. The next step involves simplifying and streamlining trade formalities, initially using paper documents but advancing to information and communication technology solutions and paperless trade systems. The final step is enabling electronic data and document exchange through national systems like the single window, allowing stakeholders in partner countries to access the information needed for efficient trade and cost reduction.[10]

---

[10] This step-by-step process is inspired by, and generally consistent with the United Nations Centre for Trade Facilitation and Electronic Business (UN/CEFACT) step-by-step approach to trade facilitation in the move toward a single window environment.

Figure 7:   Moving Up the Trade Facilitation Ladder toward Seamless International Supply Chains

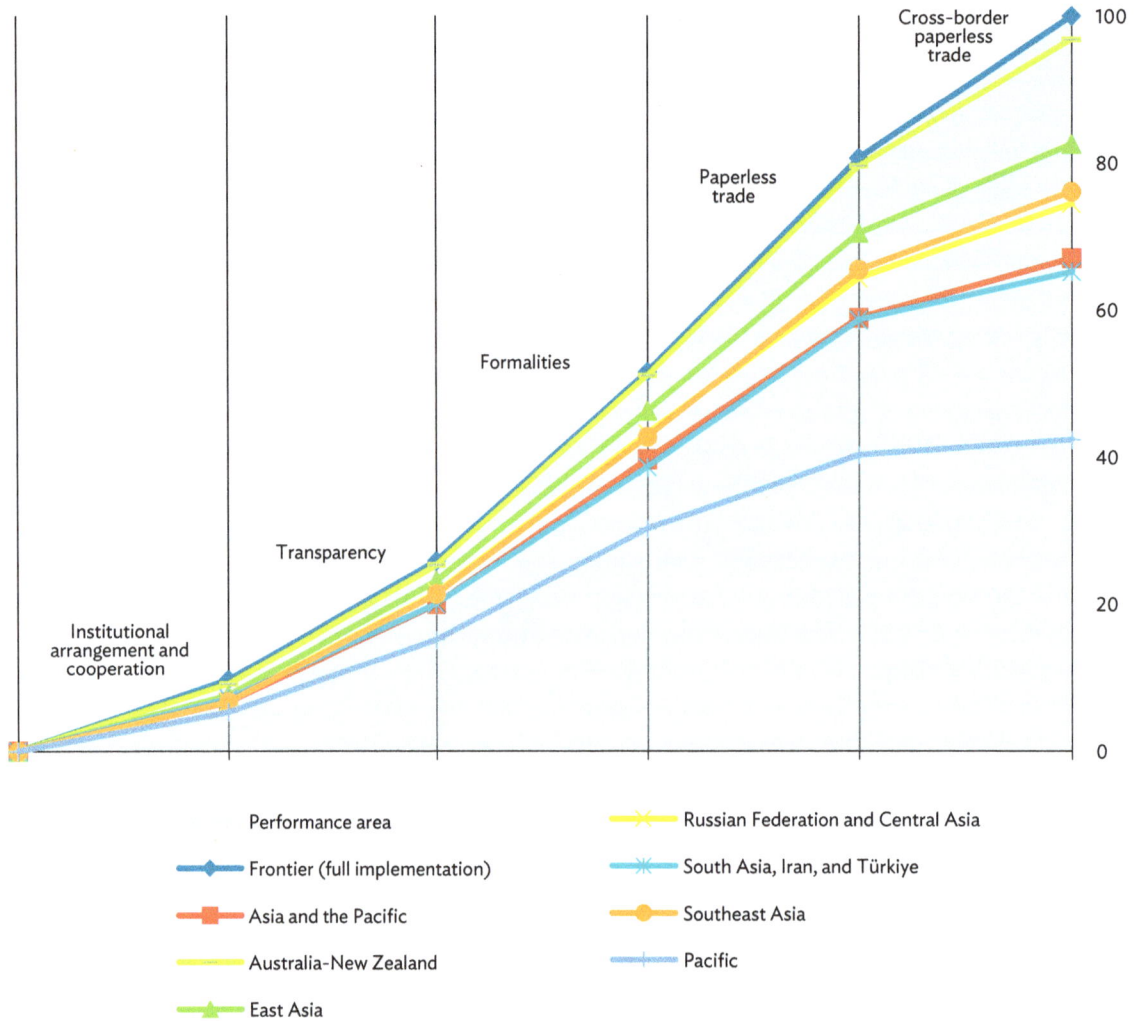

Note: The figure shows global cumulative trade facilitation implementation scores for different regions in the five subgroups of trade facilitation measures included in the survey. Scores are based on the equally weighted implementation of 31 trade facilitation measures, but the number of measures varies in the five subgroups. Full implementation of all measures = 100.

Source: United Nations (UN). UN Global Survey on Digital and Sustainable Trade Facilitation. 2023 Survey results at untfsurvey.org.

Collaboration is essential, especially concerning paperless and cross-border paperless trade, where countries need to develop and implement necessary legal and technical protocols for the seamless exchange of regulatory and commercial data and documents at national and cross-border levels. The Framework Agreement on Facilitation of Cross-Border Paperless Trade in Asia and the Pacific can serve as a dedicated, inclusive, and capacity-building intergovernmental platform to support countries in their gradual transition toward "less-paper" and eventually paperless and cross-border paperless trade, achieving trade digitalization in the Asia and Pacific region. Therefore, all countries in Asia and the Pacific are encouraged to become parties to the treaty as soon as possible to benefit from its offerings, particularly in terms of accessing capacity-building and technical assistance.

Sustainable trade facilitation represents a crucial aspect of trade facilitation. Despite its importance, the implementation of inclusive measures to promote small and medium-sized enterprises (SMEs) in trade remains very low. SMEs represent a substantial portion of the regional market and continue to encounter significant obstacles that disproportionately hinder their participation in international trade. Challenges such as inadequate access to digital infrastructure, a shortage of information technology skills, and limited financial resources hinder SMEs significantly. To achieve sustainable trade facilitation, it is crucial to prioritize building the capacity of SMEs and consider their specific needs in trade facilitation policies. Providing SMEs with the essential resources and assistance will strengthen their capacity to participate in trade, fostering a more inclusive and sustainable trade landscape.

Similarly, although significant progress has been made in implementing measures relating to "women in trade facilitation", the participation of women in trade remains low. The UN Global Survey highlights a lack of awareness regarding the importance of gender-inclusive policies in trade facilitation. Providing assistance to assist women traders in understanding trade procedures, setting up guidelines for standards bodies to guarantee fair representation of both genders' interests, and promoting women's active involvement and decision-making in trade facilitation and standards-related activities could result in significant advantages. Such an approach can potentially boost exports and create improved income opportunities for women. Recognizing the importance of these specific groups in attaining sustainable and inclusive development, trade facilitation strategies should be formulated more comprehensively and inclusively.

Moreover, results of the recently added *trade facilitation in times of crisis* subgroup show that countries are beginning to take note of the importance of long-term measures for building resiliency to pandemics and other crises. Continued endeavors are necessary to deepen cooperation, increase transparency in trade information, and adequately prepare for future crises, including the ongoing climate crisis, in which trade facilitation is set to play a significant mitigating role (ESCAP 2021).[11]

---

[11]   Pacific. 2021. Asia-Pacific Trade and Investment Report 2021: Accelerating Climate-Smart Trade and Investment for Sustainable Development.

REFERENCES

Arvis, J., et al. 2016. Trade Costs in the Developing World: 1996–2010. *World Trade Review*. 15 (3). pp. 451–474. https://www.cambridge.org/core/journals/world-trade-review/article/abs/trade-costs-in-the-developing-world-19962010/D0A95C6CF747B51FFF550B86A4C90E1C doi:10.1017/S147474561500052X.

Duval, Y., N. Prince, and C. Utoktham. 2024. Trade Digitalization Index: A New Tool for Assessing the Global State of Play in the Digitalization of Trade Procedures. Working Paper Series January 2024. Bangkok: ESCAP Trade, Investment and Innovation Division. https://www.unescap.org/kp/2024/trade-digitalization-index-new-tool-assessing-global-state-play-digitalization-trade.

Duval Y., C. Utoktham, and A. Kravchenko. 2018. Impact of Implementation of Digital Trade Facilitation on Trade Costs. ARTNeT Working Paper Series. No. 174. January 2018. Bangkok: ESCAP. https://www.unescap.org/sites/default/files/AWP174.pdf.

Economic and Social Commission for Asia and the Pacific (ESCAP). 2021. Asia-Pacific Trade and Investment Report 2021: Accelerating Climate-Smart Trade and Investment for Sustainable Development. Bangkok. https://www.unescap.org/kp/APTIR2021.

———. 2024. Digital and Sustainable Trade Facilitation: Asia-Pacific Report 2023. Bangkok.

———. n.d. Framework Agreement on Facilitation of Cross-Border Paperless Trade in Asia and the Pacific. https://www.unescap.org/kp/cpta.

United Nations. 2023. *Digital and Sustainable Trade Facilitation: Global Report 2023*. https://www.untfsurvey.org/files/documents/report-digital-sustainable-2023-global.pdf.

———. 2024. Vienna Programme of Action for Landlocked Developing Countries for the Decade 2014–2024. https://www.un.org/ohrlls/sites/www.un.org.ohrlls/files/vienna_programme_of_action.pdf.

World Trade Organization (WTO). *World Trade Report 2015*. Geneva. https://www.wto.org/english/res_e/booksp_e/world_trade_report15_e.pdf.

———. 2023. Global Trade Outlook and Statistics. Geneva. https://www.wto.org/english/res_e/booksp_e/gtos_updt_oct23_e.pdf.

PROMOTING SUSTAINABILITY AND RESILIENCE IN GLOBAL VALUE CHAINS

1 Introduction

Global value chains (GVCs) refer to the spreading of different production stages across different countries. This may include activities such as design, production, marketing, distribution, and support to the final consumer. International production, trade, and investments have been increasingly organized around GVCs. GVCs are characterized by narrow patterns of specialization—in sectors, products, tasks, and activities, accompanied by frequent movements of intermediate goods and services across borders during production.

The Asia and Pacific region has stood out in GVC development. The region's GVC trade has climbed from $621 billion in 2000 to about $3.6 trillion in 2022, while its global share of GVC trade has steadily climbed from 24% to 30% over the same period, according to the Asian Development Bank (ADB) Multiregional Input-Output table. GVC trade has underpinned rapid economic and regional trade growth within Asia and the Pacific. Breaking up production processes, which gained momentum in the early 2000s, enabled the introduction of new efficiencies and productivity gains, and made it possible for developing countries to participate and find their niche in production chains (ADB 2021). GVCs appear in sectors including apparel and footwear, automobiles, electronics, and the agro-food industry, and have supported the participation of countries of different levels of development (ESCAP 2015). Indeed, GVC trade has enabled more opportunities for productivity growth than trade in final goods and services. While countries such as the Republic of Korea industrialized by developing full supply chains in particular sectors, countries now rapidly industrializing, such as Viet Nam, are specializing in more narrowly defined tasks according to their comparative advantage.

Factors linked to cost efficiency, market access, and low international trade costs have driven the rise of GVCs. Spreading production across multiple countries is only possible in a trading environment where it is relatively easy to move goods and services across borders. Moving intermediates used in production is particularly important. While lead multinational firms allocate various stages of production to different countries to reduce production costs, intermediate goods that cross borders for further assembly may incur additional trade costs. Such costs have declined from lower transport and communications costs, as well as trade policy and trade facilitation measures. Meanwhile, the increasing trade of intermediate goods has presented new challenges for regulatory bodies, including issues related to tariffs, valuation, transfer pricing, and rules of origin of products. These challenges require special arrangements and highlight the need for enhanced trade facilitation.

As lockdowns and mobility restrictions during the coronavirus disease (COVID-19) pandemic disrupted global supply chains, they highlighted the vulnerability of supply chains and the need for resilience and sustainability. While international trade flows recovered within a year of the pandemic, other challenges developed that added to uncertainties, such as the ongoing trade tensions between the United States (US) and the People's Republic of China (PRC), the Russian invasion of Ukraine, and the more recent war in the Middle East. Moreover, the critical threat of climate change and the need to keep temperatures below the Paris Agreement threshold of 1.5 degrees above pre-industrial levels highlights the need for resilience through climate adaptation and sustainability through climate mitigation. Google Trends, for example, notes a high web search interest in supply chain sustainability since 2016, while interest in resilience spiked in 2021 during the pandemic (Box 1).

Businesses increasingly are worried about adverse weather and disasters and changing laws and regulations and politics. During the pandemic, businesses concerned about human illness as a source of supply chain disruption jumped from about 10% in 2019 to 83% in 2021, but declined to 46% in 2023 (BCI 2023) (Figure 1), and to 31% based on respondents' expectations in the next 5 years. Concerns over adverse weather steadily climbed from 35% in 2019, with expectations to increase further to 46% over the next 5 years from 2023, while concerns about disasters (e.g., tsunamis, earthquakes) jumped from 6% to 44% over the same period. Concerns over new regulations and political change also jumped, from 15% to 41% and from 10% to 36%, respectively, over the same period.

Box 1: Google Search Results for "Supply Chain Resilience", "Supply Chain Sustainability", and "Trade Facilitation"

Web search interest for supply chain sustainability has been consistently high over the 5 years through October 2023, with a notable uptick since the COVID-19 pandemic's onset (figure). However, interest in supply chain resilience, which had received little public attention for several years, surged starting in April 2021. Escalating pandemic-induced supply chain bottlenecks and growing concern for supply chain resilience likely drove this spike.

Meanwhile, data suggest that over the 5 years, trade facilitation consistently garnered public interest, and was less affected by the pandemic. In recent years, the relevance of trade facilitation to the resilience and sustainability of supply chains has increased. A correlation analysis implies an increased association between trade facilitation and supply chain sustainability and resilience in 2022. This trend subsequently decreased, but, in 2023, the measure suggests a rising trend in these correlations.

Results for Supply Chain Resilience, Supply Chain Sustainability, Trade Facilitation (latest 5 years)

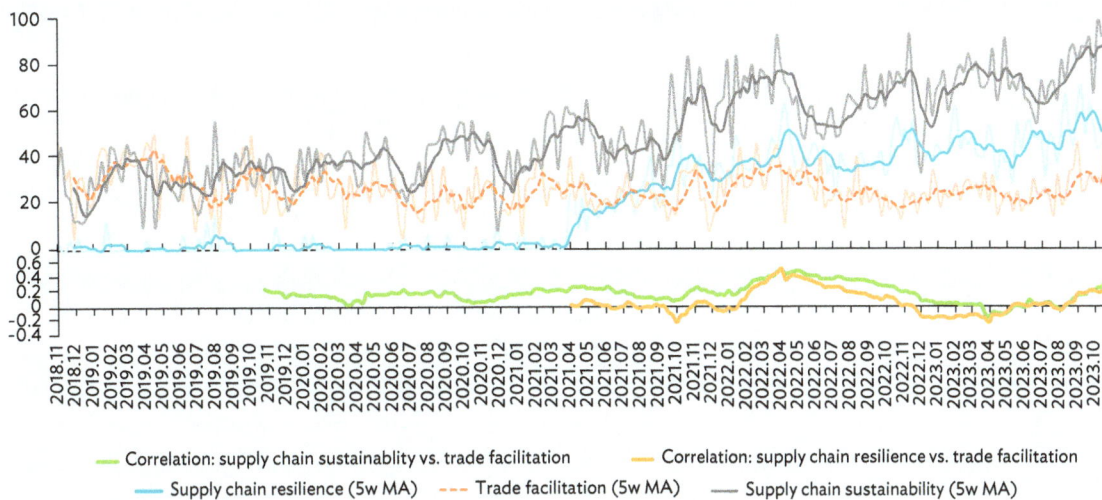

— Correlation: supply chain sustainablity vs. trade facilitation   — Correlation: supply chain resilience vs. trade facilitation
— Supply chain resilience (5w MA)   --- Trade facilitation (5w MA)   — Supply chain sustainability (5w MA)

5w MA = 5-week moving average.

Note: In the upper panel, the numbers indicate the search interest relative to the highest point on the chart within the specified region and time frame. A value of 100 represents the peak popularity of the term. In the lower panel, the two lines represent 52-week rolling window correlation coefficients.

Source: Google Trends. https://trends.google.com/trends/ (accessed 20 November 2023).

Figure 1: **Top-10 Major Sources of Supply Chain Disruption before and after COVID-19**
(% of respondents)

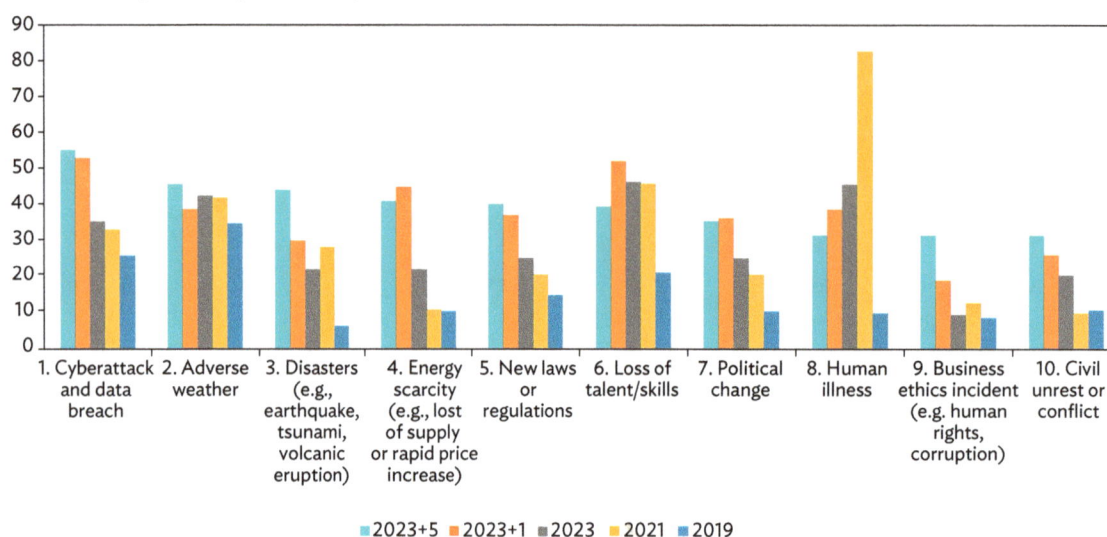

COVID-19 = coronavirus disease.
Note: +5 = prospects after 5 years; +1 = prospects after 1 year.
Source: BCI (2023).

Trade facilitation can play a key role in improving the resilience and sustainability of GVCs. Adopting digital technologies, for example, enables businesses and regulators to identify and manage risks, while enhancing transparency and simplifying and harmonizing trade procedures helps reduce trade costs and enhance GVC participation. While trade facilitation policies alone do not determine the shape of GVCs in terms of supplier sourcing arrangements, they are key factors that affect the ability of firms to move goods rapidly when needed or source them from alternative suppliers with minimum additional cost. Moreover, while only a few countries manufacture environmental goods such as solar panels and wind turbines, trade facilitation measures ensure that such goods are widely available to other countries. An integrated approach to trade and transport facilitation is also needed to enhance sustainability and decarbonization. Such an approach will reduce delays and wait times at ports, and transport also needs to transition to renewable power sources.

This chapter analyzes GVC trends and trade facilitation reforms in Asia, and provides a conceptual framework for utilizing trade facilitation to make GVCs more resilient and environment-friendly. Section 2 shows trends in GVC trade in the region, and the extent of forward and backward linkages in different sectors and subregions in Asia. It also shows the progress of implementing trade facilitation measures in the subregions in Asia, and how trade facilitation relates to GVC trade. Section 3 presents an analysis of the extent of carbon emissions embodied in production and trade in the region as well as from transport, the factors that affect GVC sustainability. Section 4 presents some recent examples of supply chain disruptions in essential goods such as personal protective equipment, vaccines, and agricultural goods, and how these were addressed during the pandemic. Trends in supply chain pressures are also shown, while factors that determine supply chain resilience are discussed. Section 5 presents an analytical framework on how various aspects of sustainability and resilience of supply chains discussed in Sections 3 and 4 relate to trade facilitation measures. Section 6 concludes with policy considerations.

2 Background

2.1 | GVC Trade and Participation in Asia and the Pacific

GVCs can be measured by breaking down gross exports into three components: domestic value added, foreign value added, and pure double counting (Wang, Wei, and Zhu 2013). Domestic value added is the part of gross exports in which value added originates in the exporting country. Foreign value added, by contrast, is the part of gross exports in which value added originates in foreign countries. Pure double counting indicates movements of goods and services back and forth across borders, and highlights instances where conventional trade data are recording transactions multiple times during production. A higher share of foreign value added in gross exports means that a country is sourcing inputs from abroad more intensively to produce its exports, which is consistent with a greater degree of GVC integration through backward linkages, while a larger share of domestic value added denotes more domestically sourced inputs, indicating forward linkages in GVCs.

The Asia and Pacific region has been a standout performer in GVC development over recent decades. While the region's share of total trade rose from 25% to 33% during 2000–2022, total trade quintupled from $1.8 trillion to $9.9 trillion in that period (Figure 2a). GVC trade increased nearly sixfold from about $621 billion in 2000 to $3.6 trillion in 2022, and its global share of GVC trade rose steadily from 24% to 30% (Figure 2b). Indeed, GVC development was significant in Asia and the Pacific in the 1990s, 2000s, and onward, and remains so.

Figure 2: Total Trade and GVC Trade, 2000–2022 ($ billion)

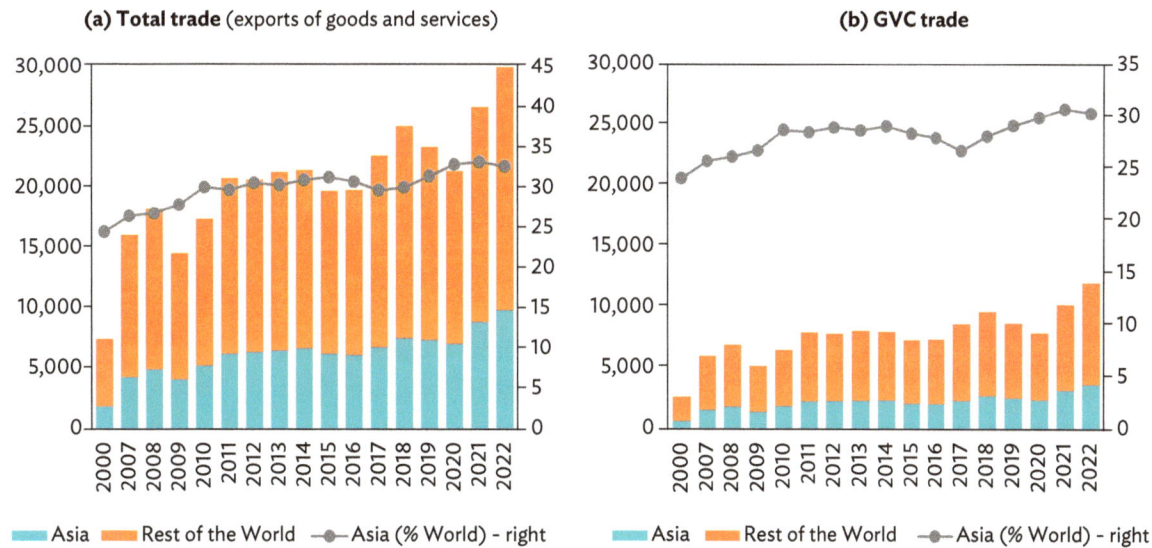

(a) Total trade (exports of goods and services)

(b) GVC trade

Legend: Asia — Rest of the World — Asia (% World) - right

GVC = global value chain.

Note: GVC trade is gross exports that involves production in at least two economies using cross-border production networks.

Source: Authors' calculations based on ADB Multiregional Input–Output Tables. https://kidb.adb.org/mrio (accessed 24 November 2023).

The shares of backward and forward linkages in the region's GVC trade are similar, but the nature of GVC participation varies considerably from one subregion to another. The share of backward linkages increased slightly from 17% to 20% during 2000–2022, while the share of forward linkages remained flat at about 17% during the period (Figure 3a). Higher backward linkage implies the important role that regional and global sourcing of inputs plays in Asia and Pacific countries, and is a key feature of the GVC business model in the region. Southeast Asia is overall the most GVC-integrated subregion in Asia and the Pacific, while South Asia is the least (Figure 3b). Whereas backward linkages dominate in Southeast Asia and the Pacific, forward linkages are relatively more important in Central Asia and Oceania. In part, this result reflects different patterns of sectoral specialization, given its association with GVC participation: extractive industries such as mining and petroleum typically produce exports of commodities that are used by other countries to produce other goods and services; these industries are significant in the latter two regions. Primary sectors tend to focus relatively more heavily on forward linkages, whereas manufacturing generally has a strong role for backward linkages (Figure 4). Such differences can play out at the country level, given that patterns of sectoral specialization differ.

Although landlocked countries show a higher level of GVCs compared to coastal countries, their reliance on forward linkages highlights distinct variations in how they are integrated and the specific challenges they face. Landlocked countries are more integrated into GVCs than coastal countries (41.6% of gross export value versus 35.4%, respectively). But the balance between backward and forward linkages is very different. Backward linkages dominate in coastal countries (19.6% of gross export value) but forward linkages are strongly dominant in landlocked countries (32.3%% of gross export value). Sectoral specialization plays into this result, and reflects the difficulty of setting up multinational production platforms in landlocked countries, and potentially geography and policy-related difficulties in moving goods easily across borders (Borchert et al. 2017). Landlocked countries' greater integration into GVCs and reliance on forward linkages underscore the necessity of efficient transit routes, regional cooperation, and strategic policy reforms for enhancing trade facilitation.

2.2 | Tracking Trade Facilitation in Asia and the Pacific

The objective of trade facilitation is to reduce trade costs, which encompass the full range of factors that drive a wedge between producer prices in an exporting country and consumer prices in an importing country (Anderson and Van Wincoop 2004). This idea includes policy-related barriers, such as tariffs or poor trade facilitation, as well as geographic and historical factors that make it harder for countries to trade, the cost and reliability of transport linkages between countries (including transport facilitation), and the possibility of engaging in digital transactions.

Trade facilitation and trade costs have been conceptualized in a "broad" and "narrow" sense. In its early work on trade facilitation, the Asia-Pacific Economic Cooperation (APEC) envisaged "trade facilitation" as the broad set of policies ranging from border procedures to the administration of nontariff measures, to "behind the border" barriers such as the business environment and investment climate. An alternative approach to trade facilitation is typified by the World Trade Organization (WTO) Trade Facilitation Agreement (TFA). It focuses on reducing trade costs exclusively through the rationalization of customs and border procedures, including through reductions in paperwork, facilitation of information flow, institutional upgrading, and streamlining of processes. This approach to trade facilitation is narrower than the APEC approach, but has the advantage of being backed by an important international legal instrument in the form of the TFA, which is now part of the corpus of WTO law.

Figure 3: GVC Participation, Asia

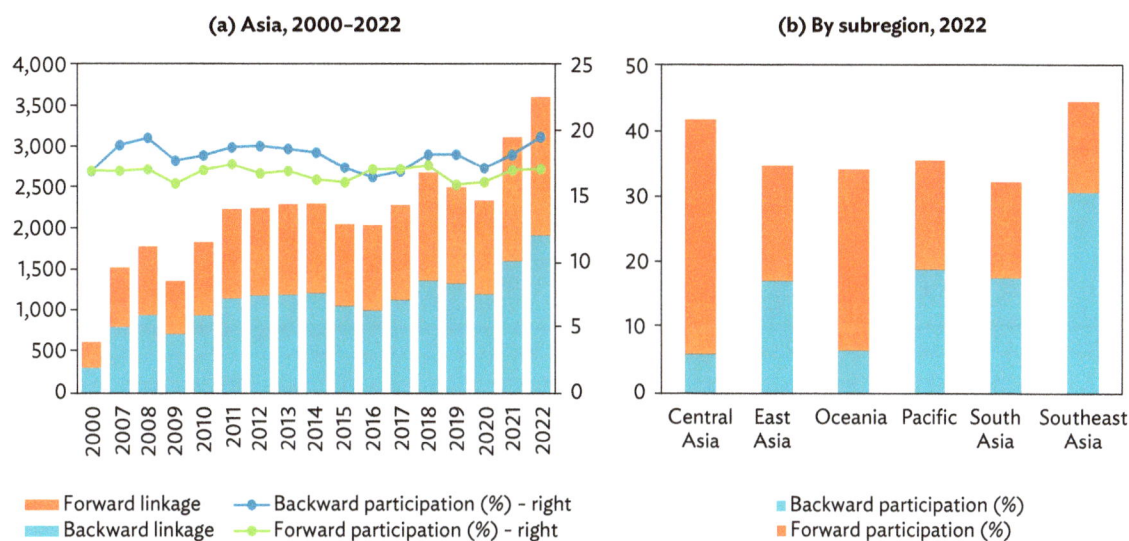

(a) Asia, 2000–2022

(b) By subregion, 2022

Forward linkage — Backward participation (%) - right
Backward linkage — Forward participation (%) - right

Backward participation (%)
Forward participation (%)

GVC = global value chain.

Note: The GVC participation rate is the share of gross exports that involves production in at least two economies using cross-border production networks. Backward and forward participation rates are in % of gross export value.

Source: Authors' calculations based on ADB Multiregional Input–Output Tables. https://kidb.adb.org/mrio (accessed 24 November 2023).

Figure 4: Global Value Chain Participation by Merchandise Sector, 2022

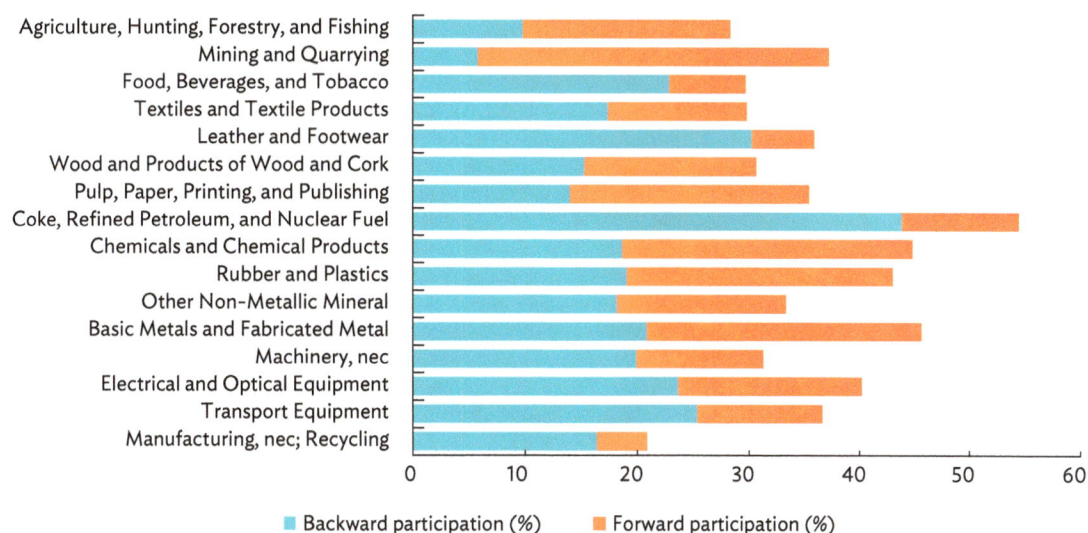

Backward participation (%)   Forward participation (%)

nec = not elsewhere classified.

Note: The global value chain participation rate is the share of gross exports that involves production in at least two economies using cross-border production networks. Backward and forward participation rates are in % of gross export value.

Source: Authors' calculations based on ADB Multiregional Input–Output Tables . https://kidb.adb.org/mrio (accessed 24 November 2023).

Two main international datasets track implementation of trade facilitation policies in a practical sense. The Organisation for Economic Co-operation and Development (OECD) Trade Facilitation Indicators (TFIs) provide comparable data from 2017 through 2022 at 2- to 3-year intervals, covering 11 performance pillars. Each pillar is based on a range of detailed indicators collected by the OECD including through consultations with governments. The UN Global Survey on Digital and Sustainable Trade Facilitation (DSTF) has a similar objective—tracking performance on a wide range of detailed policy indicators—and aggregates expert survey responses into scores across nine pillars. Compared with the OECD indicators, it puts more emphasis on paperless trade and on non-trade objectives such as SME development, agriculture, and gender inclusiveness. It covers 2015–2023 at 2-year intervals.

Trade facilitation performance in all subregions has been improving (Figure 5). The two sources display exactly the same ordering of average performance across subregions, from Oceania in the lead to the Pacific in the tail. This finding is remarkably robust, given that the data are compiled from different sources, in different ways, and with differing points of emphasis and extension. The evidence on ordering of performance across subregions is therefore very strong. Similarly, they agree that landlocked countries generally display weaker performance than coastal countries: 0.6 versus 0.7 for the DSTF and 1.1 versus 1.3 for the TFIs. These two data sources confirm the difficulties landlocked countries face in accessing global markets.

The TFIs suggest that external and internal cooperation, as well as automation, are areas in which at least some subregions see particular issues. Breaking out the two indicators by pillar does not change the ordering of subregions radically (Figure 6). While the pillars differ in each case, the ordering of subregions is consistent across them. However, the figure clearly shows that average performance levels are stronger or weaker in particular areas. The DSTF data, on the other hand, highlight gender, SMEs, and cross-border paperless trade as areas where most subregions display performance deficits.

Figure 5: **Average Trade Facilitation Performance, by Asia and Pacific Subregion, 2017–2022**

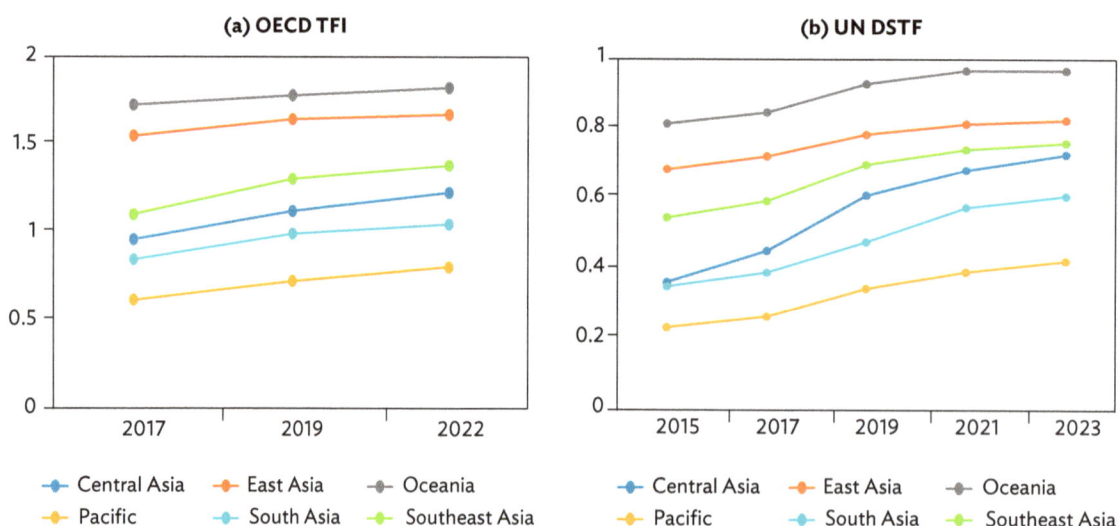

DSTF = Digital and Sustainable Trade Facilitation, OECD = Organisation for Economic Co-operation and Development, TFI = trade facilitation indicator, UN = United Nations.
Sources: OECD Trade Facilitation Indicators; UN Global Survey on Digital and Sustainable Trade Facilitation. untfsurvey.org.

Figure 6: Average Trade Facilitation Pillar Performance, by Asia and Pacific Subregion

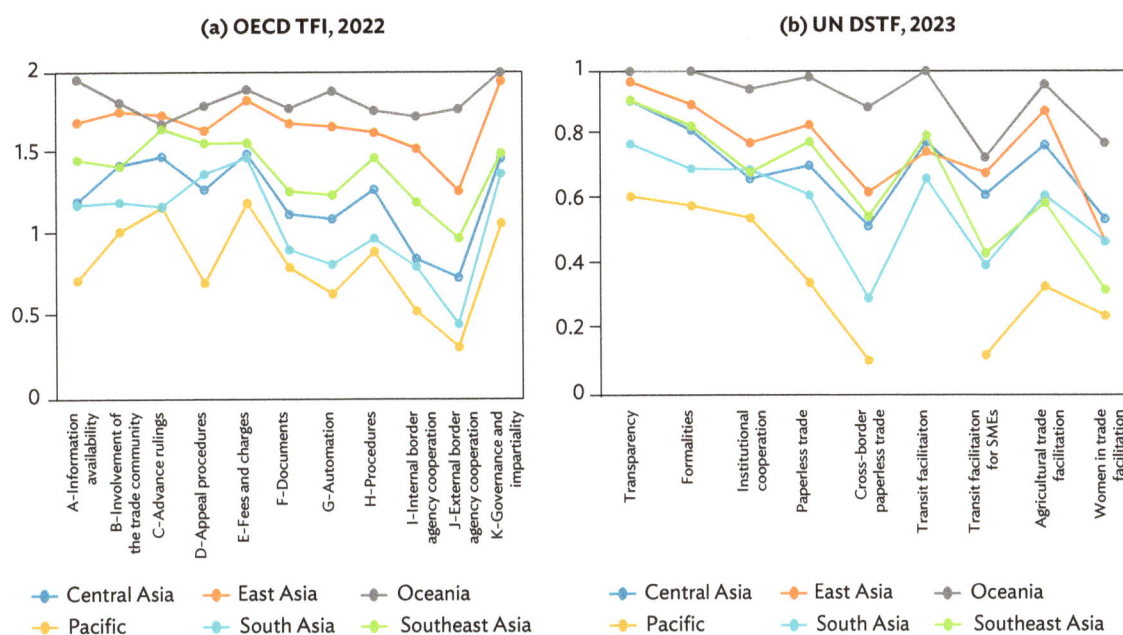

(a) OECD TFI, 2022

(b) UN DSTF, 2023

Central Asia   East Asia   Oceania
Pacific   South Asia   Southeast Asia

Central Asia   East Asia   Oceania
Pacific   South Asia   Southeast Asia

DSTF = Digital and Sustainable Trade Facilitation, OECD = Organisation for Economic Co-operation and Development, TFI = trade facilitation indicator, SMEs = small and medium-sized enterprises, UN = United Nations.

Sources: OECD Trade Facilitation Indicators; UN Global Survey on Digital and Sustainable Trade Facilitation. untfsurvey.org.

2.3 | Trade Facilitation–GVC Nexus

In the current global trading environment, ability to move goods and services across borders easily — especially production intermediates—is crucial. This ease of trade has been a key factor in the Asia and Pacific region's successful use of GVCs as a development engine. Different sectors face unique challenges in meeting regulatory requirements and ensuring rapid, cost-effective border crossings. For example, perishable goods and complex machinery components are time sensitive and require special handling (Hummels and Schaur 2013). Logistics performance is critical for products like vaccines, which need cold chain storage and delicate handling (Helble and Shepherd 2017). However, as risks such as climate change and geopolitical tensions increasingly affect trade costs, determining the right policies to facilitate trade has become a primary concern in trade policy. With the reduction of tariff rates worldwide, the focus of policymaking has shifted toward addressing other trade barriers. Policymakers are also increasingly looking at trade as a means to achieve broader policy objectives, including those related to environmental and social sustainability.

The importance of trade facilitation is increasingly evident for GVC trade dynamics. The complexity of GVCs often involves multiple border crossings, which may increase trade costs, such as higher tariffs, border taxes, transportation, insurance expenses, and unaligned regulatory measures (Jones, Demirkaya, and, Bethmann 2019). This complexity can reduce the expected benefits of GVC participation. Empirical studies indicate that these additional costs can increase production expenses by 18% (Escaith 2017) and elevate ad valorem trade costs by 10%–30% by having more stages in the chain (Ferrantino 2012). Further, nontariff measures like licensing requirements and technical standards can act as barriers, escalating trade costs during the progression of GVCs.

The activities facilitating trade significantly impact various stages of GVCs, including raw materials sourcing, production, assembly, and logistics (Table 1). Customs procedures are pivotal in stages where the physical movement of goods occurs, while institutional arrangements and cooperation refer to national trade facilitation committees that coordinate with each other to share best practices and coordinate toward trade policy harmonization. Paperless trade gets rid of manual processes and wet signatures and helps to enhance efficiency and security. Trade policies influence all stages of GVCs and are important in the design stage to protect intellectual property while promoting market access. Trade finance is used in about 80% of trade flows and is crucial for procuring raw materials, production, and expanding market reach. Information and communication technology significantly helps all stages of trade procedures to work together seamlessly including coordination, design, production monitoring, marketing, and customer service. Meanwhile, transportation is critical in stages that involve the physical movement of goods, especially in multiple border crossings.

Table 1: Potential Trade Facilitation Impact on Global Value Chain Stages

Trade Facilitation Elements\GVC Stages	R&D	Design	Raw Material Sourcing	Production	Assembly	Logistics	Marketing and Sales	After-Sales Services
Customs procedures	Low	Low	High	High	High	High	Moderate	Low
Institutional arrangement and cooperation	Low	Low	High	Moderate	High	High	Low	Low
Trade policies	Moderate	High	High	High	High	High	High	Moderate
Transport facilitation	Low	Moderate	High	High	High	Very High	High	Moderate
Paperless trade facilitation	Low	Low	High	High	High	High	Moderate	Low
Access to trade finance	Moderate	Moderate	High	High	High	High	High	Low
IT and communication	High	High	Moderate	High	High	High	High	High

GVC = global value chain, IT = information technology, R&D = research and development.
Source: Authors.

Indeed, a substantial body of research finds the significant role of trade facilitation in boosting GVC trade, highlighting transparency, modernization, and automation. Martínez-Zarzoso (2023) found that better trade facilitation is associated with higher GVC trade, with institutions and cross-border trade facilitation playing major roles. Engman (2005) similarly identified that initiatives in customs modernization can help developing countries participate in the international supply chain, particularly for industries engaged in intermediate industrial components and time-sensitive goods and products. Looking at Sub-Saharan Africa, Takpara, Djiogap, and Sawagodo (2023) found that trade facilitation indicators such as infrastructure and information and communication technology matter most for countries to participate in the GVC trade for agriculture, manufacturing, and textiles and clothing sectors. Dong (2021) also concluded that trade facilitation can influence the density of the trade network. Moise and Sorescu (2015) found that the most important factor in terms of how efficiently a country can conduct GVC trade are streamlining of border procedures and controls; proportionality and transparency of import and export fees and charges; and automation of border processes. An exercise using correlation coefficients between trade facilitation performance indicators and GVC participation confirms a generally positive association between these variables (Figure 7). The degree of association varies by specific trade facilitation measures, aligning with existing literature that underscores the importance of efficiency in trade procedures.

The literature also suggests that trade facilitation may impact trade in intermediate goods differently compared to final goods. Saslavsky and Shepherd (2012) found that trade in parts and components is more sensitive to changes in trade facilitation measures compared to trade in final goods. Similarly, Shepherd (2022) illustrated that trade facilitation measures can have different effects depending on end use and sectors. Estimated elasticities for mining and quarrying, machinery, and electrical and optical equipment are larger for intermediates than final goods, implying that trade in intermediates in these sectors are more affected by improvements in trade facilitation. Hummels and Schaur (2013) found that trade in intermediate goods is time-sensitive such that the cost of a one-day delay in transit is 60% higher for importers of intermediate goods than for importers of final goods.

Figure 7: Correlation between Trade Facilitation Performance and GVC Participation, World, 2022

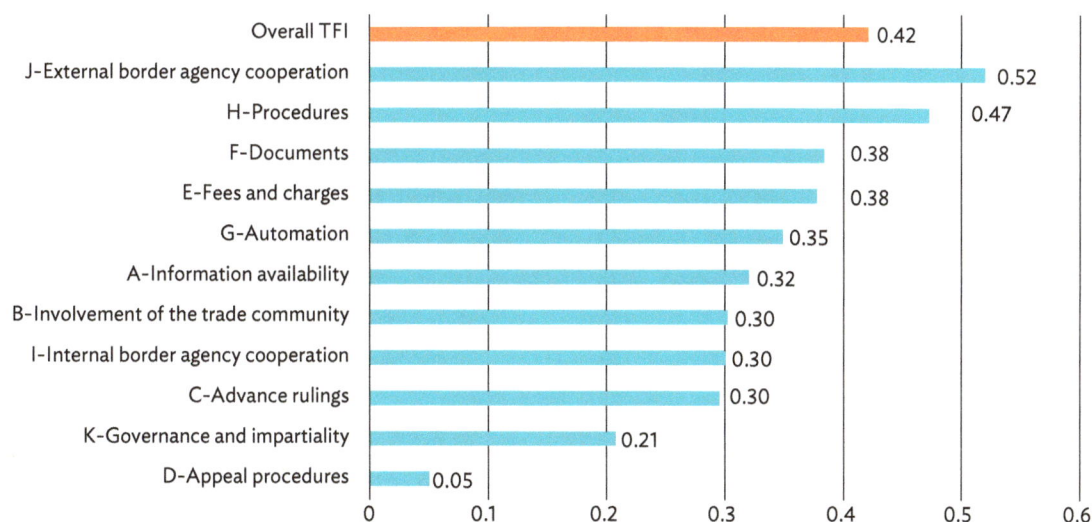

GVC = global value chain, TFI = trade facilitation indicator.

Note: The correlation coefficients are calculated using the log of the average trade facilitation indicator and the global value chain (GVC) participation rate in percentage. Each trade facilitation indicator indicates the following: A-Information Availability: Ensuring access to trade-related information, including online; B-Involvement of the trade community: Engaging traders in policymaking and providing frameworks for feedback; C-Advance rulings: Offering prior determinations on classifications, origins, and valuation methods for imported goods; D-Appeal procedures: Providing mechanisms to challenge administrative decisions by border agencies; E-Fees and charges: Regulating fees and penalties associated with imports and exports; F-Documents: Simplifying and standardizing trade documents, including accepting copies; G-Automation: Implementing electronic data exchange and automated processes in border procedures; H-Procedures: Streamlining border controls and introducing efficient documentation processes like single submission points; I-Internal border agency cooperation: Facilitating collaboration and control delegation among domestic border agencies; J-External border agency cooperation: Encouraging cooperation with border agencies of neighboring and third countries; and K-Governance and impartiality: Ensuring ethical, accountable, and efficient customs structures and functions.

Sources: Asian Development Bank Multiregional Input-Output tables, OECD Trade Facilitation Indicators.

3 Sustainability in Global Value Chains

3.1 | Background: Carbon Emissions Embodied in Trade

While Asia's carbon dioxide (CO_2) emissions from production have accelerated, emissions from trade, particularly exports, have grown even more rapidly. Globally, CO_2 emissions from production increased by about 60% from 1995 to 2018, while trade-related emissions doubled during the same period (Figure 8a).[1] In Asia and the Pacific, CO_2 emissions grew around 150% for production and 250% for exports, while emissions embodied in imports increased at a rate similar to that of production-based emissions (Figure 8b). Accordingly, the share of Asia's CO_2 emissions embodied in exports relative to its production-based CO_2 emissions rose from 22% in 1995 to 31% in 2018, peaking at 36% in 2008. Asia and the Pacific has consistently been a net exporter of CO_2 emissions, with the rest of the world a net importer. Asia's consistent position as a net CO_2 emissions exporter shows its role as a major provider of goods to serve global demand, as well as its reliance on carbon-intensive manufacturing exports rather than on exports from primary and services sectors.

The region's export of manufactures accounts for 75% of CO_2 emissions embodied in exports in 2018 (Figure 9a). The trend is also reflected in various subregions: manufacturing is the main export sector in East Asia (84% of embodied CO_2 emissions in exports), South Asia (75%), and Southeast Asia (57%) (Figure 9b). Transportation services on the other hand account for 23% of embodied emissions in exports in Southeast Asia and 9% in East Asia.

When it comes to GVC trade, exports of intermediates have been more carbon intensive than exports of final goods (Figure 10). By analogy with trade in value added, which makes it possible to identify domestic and foreign sourced value added in gross exports, similar calculations allow separation of domestic and foreign origin carbon dioxide emissions contained in gross exports. There is thus empirical potential for decarbonization efforts to impact trade in intermediates more heavily than trade in final goods, which in turn would put pressure on the GVC production model.

---

[1] In this chapter, CO_2 emissions data are sourced from the $TeCO_2$ database of the Organisation for Economic Co-operation and Development (OECD). This database encompasses 19 Asia and Pacific economies, including Australia; Brunei Darussalam; Cambodia; the PRC; Hong Kong, China; India; Indonesia; Japan; Kazakhstan; the Republic of Korea; the Lao People's Democratic Republic; Malaysia; Myanmar; New Zealand; the Philippines; Singapore; Taipei,China; Thailand; and Viet Nam.

Figure 8: Trend of Carbon Dioxide Emissions, Production vs. Trade (1995 = 100)

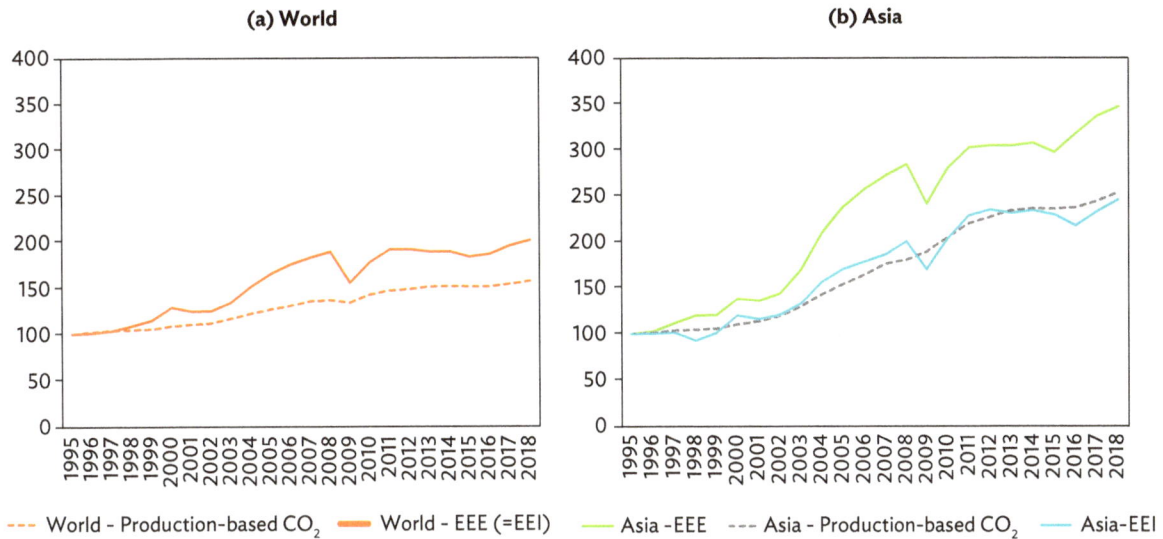

(a) World

(b) Asia

- - - World – Production-based CO_2 ——— World – EEE (=EEI)   ——— Asia –EEE   - - - Asia – Production-based CO_2 ——— Asia-EEI

CO_2 = carbon dioxide, EEE = emissions embodied in exports; EEI = emissions embodied in imports.

Source: Organisation for Economic Co-operation and Development. 2021. Trade in embodied CO_2 (TeCO_2) Database. https://www.oecd.org/industry/ind/carbondioxideemissionsembodiedininternationaltrade.htm (accessed 27 November 2023).

Figure 9: Asia's Carbon Dioxide Emissions Embodied in Exports, 2018

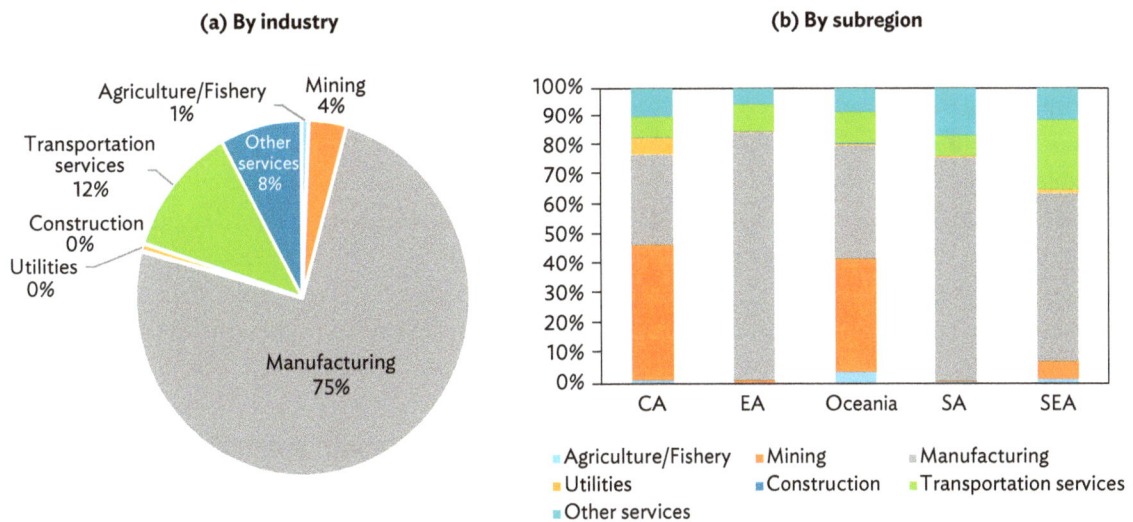

(a) By industry

(b) By subregion

- Agriculture/Fishery   - Mining   - Manufacturing
- Utilities   - Construction   - Transportation services
- Other services

CA = Central Asia, EA = East Asia, SA = South Asia, SEA = Southeast Asia.

Source: Organisation for Economic Co-operation and Development. 2021. Trade in embodied CO_2 (TeCO_2) Database. https://www.oecd.org/industry/ind/carbondioxideemissionsembodiedininternationaltrade.htm (accessed 27 November 2023).

Figure 10: Average Carbon Dioxide Intensity by Type of Trade, Asia, 2010–2018
(tons of CO_2 per \$ million)

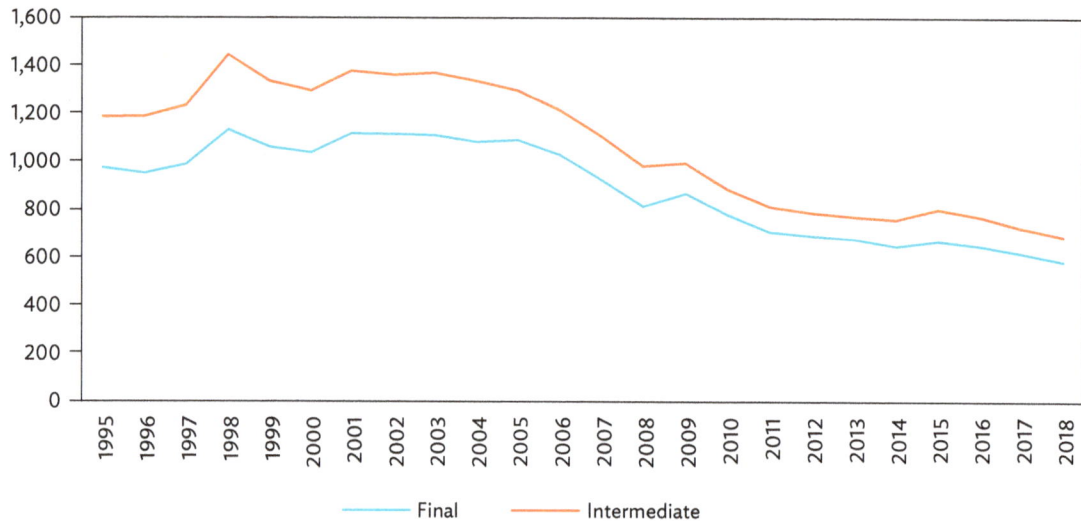

CO_2 = carbon dioxide, OECD = Organisation for Economic Co-operation and Development.

Note: Intensity of CO_2 emissions embodied in total gross exports of final (intermediate) products = CO_2 emissions embodied in total gross exports of final (intermediate) products/total gross exports value of final (intermediate) products.

Source: Author's calculations based on Organisation for Economic Co-operation and Development. 2021. Trade in embodied CO_2 (TeCO$_2$) Database. https://www.oecd.org/industry/ind/carbondioxideemissionsembodiedininternationaltrade.htm (accessed 27 November 2023).

Meanwhile, the transportation services sector ranks as the second-highest source of trade-related CO_2 emissions, accounting for 12% of the total. The International Transport Forum (ITF) report (ITF 2021) highlights that over 40% of emissions in the transportation services sector stem from trade activities, covering both domestic and international freight. In 2020, road transport was responsible for the largest portion, constituting 45% of emissions across all transport methods (Figure 11). Yet, when looking at freight activity measured in tonne-kilometers, it accounts for only about 15% (Figure 12). Meanwhile, sea transport causes only 17% of total freight emissions but handles 70% of the total freight activity, highlighting its large capacity and low carbon intensity.

Among all transport modes, air freight shows the highest carbon intensity, generating emissions 20 times higher per tonne-kilometer than the average for the entire freight sector (Figure 13). In contrast, the maritime sector boasts the lowest carbon intensity. While air cargo ensures quicker deliveries, it generally comes at a higher cost than maritime cargo, which remains a cost-effective choice for bulkier and heavier consignments. Urban freight comes next to air transport, often involving multiple trips with smaller payloads. Meanwhile, the rail transport carbon footprint is notably low.

Figure 11: Carbon Dioxide Emissions from Freight Activity by Transport Mode, 2020 (% share total)

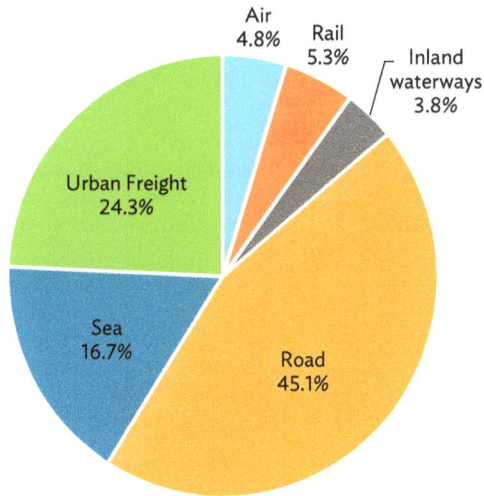

Air 4.8%
Rail 5.3%
Inland waterways 3.8%
Urban Freight 24.3%
Sea 16.7%
Road 45.1%

Note: Freight includes both domestic and international shipping.
Source: International Transport Forum (2021).

Figure 12: Freight Activity by Transport Mode, 2020 (% share total based on tonne-kilometers)

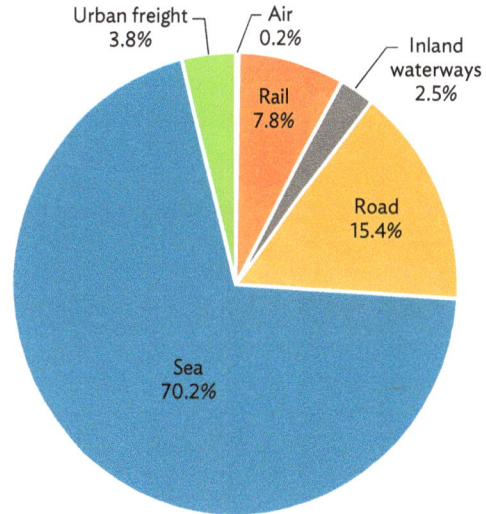

Urban freight 3.8%
Air 0.2%
Rail 7.8%
Inland waterways 2.5%
Road 15.4%
Sea 70.2%

Note: Freight includes both domestic and international shipping.
Source: International Transport Forum (2021).

Figure 13: Carbon Emissions Intensity by Transport Mode (grams of CO_2 per tonne-kilometer)

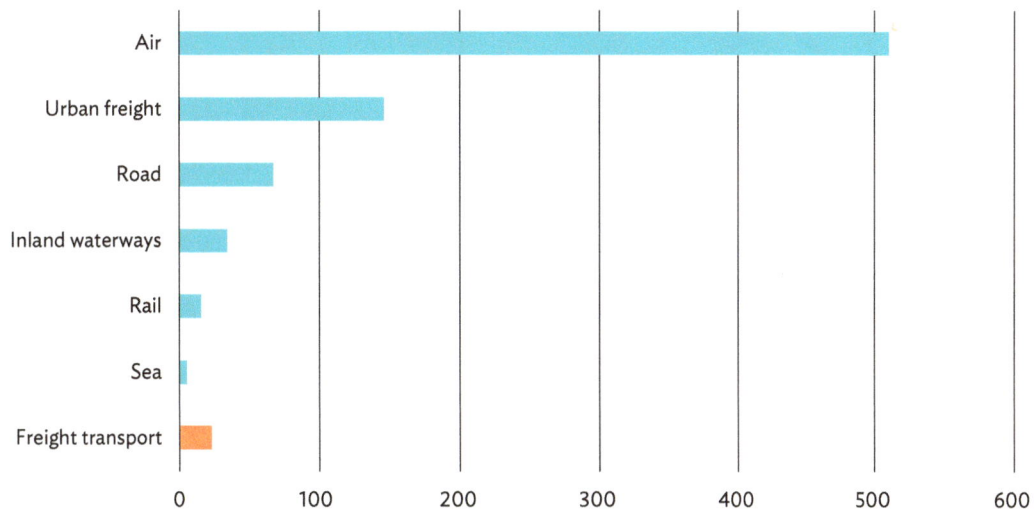

Air, Urban freight, Road, Inland waterways, Rail, Sea, Freight transport

Source: International Transport Forum (2021).

However, international transport sectors face significant challenges such as slow development of carbon-neutral freight solutions, difficulties transitioning to renewable energy sources, and the need for advanced ship design to accommodate alternative fuels and enhance efficiency (ITF 2021). In addition, the need is pressing to eliminate fossil fuel tax exemptions and incorporate freight transport emissions into carbon pricing schemes. International agreements, such as the Paris Agreement, show limitations, particularly in excluding maritime and aviation emissions.

The need to reduce CO_2 emissions provides both challenges and opportunities for GVCs in Asia and the Pacific. On the one hand, electrification and renewable energy represent major commercial outlets where GVC production methods could help reconcile sustainability goals and economic efficiency. Electric vehicles (EVs) provide a good example. The European Union and the United States both have substantial and growing EV manufacturing and assembly capacity, as does the People's Republic of China (PRC). But all manufacturers of EVs rely heavily on battery suppliers, which are largely based in the PRC with inputs from Japan and the Republic of Korea, and raw materials from a range of countries including Australia (IEA 2022). While policy measures can affect this structure, the emerging business reality of EV production is that GVCs remain relevant, as they have historically been in the production of traditional motor vehicles over recent decades.

The potential impact of decarbonization on trade costs, particularly energy prices, could significantly influence GVCs. GVCs are intimately tied to trade and transport costs, as well as the costs of imported raw materials and component parts. In the short term, decarbonization would likely increase energy prices, and thus the prices of goods and services that are relatively energy intensive; however, the effect is likely to be relatively short lived, as generation costs using renewable energy sources are typically lower than using fossil fuels once the investment costs of establishing infrastructure have been sunk; costs are declining over time (IRENA 2021). Will these kinds of cost increases undo the GVC development that has been seen around the world in the era of ultra-low trade and transaction costs, and in particular in Asia and the Pacific? Unraveling GVCs would be most likely to happen if trade costs affecting intermediates rise by substantially more than trade costs affecting final goods (e.g., Shepherd 2022). As yet, there is little evidence that such a dynamic has indeed been set in motion by efforts to decarbonize the economy, but neither can it be ruled out.

3.2 | Factors Affecting GVC Sustainability

The literature on GVCs has evolved from governance and economic upgrading to social and environmental sustainability[2] (Bair 2005; Barrientos, Gereffi, and Rossie 2021; Krishnan, De Marchi, and Ponte 2022). Supply chain disruptions induced by the pandemic have revived discussions about the sustainability of GVCs. This refers to the long-term viability of processes, including economic, social, and environmental (Blumenschein et al. 2017). This section focuses on environmental facets of sustainability through the concept of circularity.[3] This is in turn influenced by factors such as supply chain transparency and traceability, environmental standards, carbon footprint management, and green manufacturing, among others.

---

[2]   GVC governance involves a mix of trade and investment policies, regulatory frameworks, and sector-focused partnerships and agreements that enhance regional strengths, contributing to a country's trade indicators like GVC integration, value added, and overall economic performance, including GDP growth and sector productivity. Economic upgrading involves advancing to higher-value activities through product and process improvements, incorporating, for instance, interventions like technical support, certification standards, stringent supplier requirements, technology development, and training to enhance product quality and align with international standards.

[3]   A circular economy is a closed-looped production system that is based on principles of eliminating waste and pollution, reusing and recycling products and materials (Ellen MacArthur Foundation 2019).

3.2.1 Supply chain transparency and traceability, and sustainable sourcing and material use

Supply chain traceability is an important tool that provides information on the components of products, their parts and materials, and how they were transformed throughout the value chain. Traceability can thus verify and authenticate sustainability claims by providing the ability to trace back the history of the product, in turn encouraging good practices (Schröder 2008). Moreover, traceability can act as a key element in a circular supply chain where information about post-sale and post-use phases are made available for reuse, remanufacture, or recycle (WEF 2021).

Adopting digital technologies such as radio-frequency identification (known as RFID) tags to supply chain traceability helps reduce transport costs. For example, Decker et al. (2008) showed that by closely monitoring the product conditions within vehicles (i.e., right temperature for fresh foods), costs associated with product return, removal, and disposal due to inappropriate handling can be cut down. A geographic information system can also provide production information for agricultural products, such as the place, fertilizer management, and use of pesticides, which are all visualized in the whole supply chain management system (Deng et al. 2008). Emerging technologies include big data and analytics, which enable the analysis of huge volumes of information and help to identify inefficiencies, while the Internet of Things facilitates the exchange of data between systems. Artificial intelligence and machine learning help automate processes, while blockchain technology provides a secure database that records every transaction as well as real-time tracking and traceability of products (Ashcroft 2023).

Traceability in supply chains encourages transparency and reduces vulnerability. Greater traceability incentivizes firms to be more transparent with consumers and stakeholders, because it will be able to pinpoint locations as well as suppliers that integrate environmental upgrading in their operations. A study by Hamprecht et al. (2005) on Nestlé's quality control and sustainable management, for instance, integrates traceability in their supply chain. Using this, the company records and monitors its suppliers' activities (i.e., dairy farmers), requiring them to calculate nutrition demands of the soil, to make sure that their farming practices are not degrading the environment.

3.2.2 Environmental standards compliance

Establishing regulations and standards to achieve sustainability goals within the GVC framework is becoming more important. Companies are also facing increasing pressure to comply with environmental sustainability requirements as part of their participation in GVCs and encourage them to provide greener and low-carbon products. In the agricultural value chain, exporters of horticultural crops from Africa to high-income markets are required to meet international certification standards. For instance, Kenyan flower companies and the Ugandan floriculture sector have upgraded their processes to meet environmental international standards for their exports (Barrientos 2014). In Ghana, the Samartex Timber and Plywood company engaged the Global Forest and Trade Network to be certified as the first sustainable timber supplier (Kaplinsky and Morris 2014). In turn, the company was able to significantly decrease its environmental impact by improving its hauling practices and educated the community on sustainable forestry practices.

3.2.3 Others: Green manufacturing, carbon footprint management, and energy efficiency

Environmental sustainability is reflected in the supply chain management literature through ecological efficiency and environmental risk reduction (Govindan et al. 2015; Geng, Mansouri, and Aktas 2017; Rupa and Saif 2021). In a study of the equipment manufacturing industry in the PRC, Li et al. (2022) found that GVC upgrading through green technology innovation can reduce pollution costs and promote green products. Beheshtinia and Fathi (2022) also showed that optimizing supply chain scheduling minimized fuel consumption of vehicles and energy consumption of supplies, leading to lower carbon dioxide emissions.

4 Resilience in GVCs

4.1 | Background: Recent Supply Chain Pressures and Disruptions

Unlike previous events such as disasters triggered by natural hazards, financial crises, and epidemics, which had localized or more gradual impacts on supply chains, the impact of the COVID-19 pandemic was immediate and global. Economies implemented drastic lockdowns and mobility restrictions that hurt trade and supply chains, incomes, and employment, and caused hunger. The pandemic exposed the vulnerabilities of globalization and global supply chains. A survey of firms by BCI (2020) notes that global supply chains were tested during the pandemic more than many organizations had ever experienced in their lifetimes. As the pandemic hit, 73% of businesses noted some or significant detrimental effect on the supply side, while about 65% did so on the demand side.

At the onset of the pandemic, an abrupt global surge in demand for personal protective equipment led to protectionist measures by governments to deal with production constraints. Surging demand for surgical masks created a shortage in nonwoven polypropylene, a key material used to filter out germs and droplets. Prices of personal protective equipment products rose dramatically, by sixfold for surgical masks, threefold for respirators, and twofold for medical gowns (ADB and ESCAP 2021). While production constraints eventually eased for critical medical goods as a whole, it also led to a rethinking of supply chains, such as the geographic concentration of manufacturers in countries including the PRC, which produced half the global supply of masks, as well as trade restrictions and export bans and transport and shipping constraints.

Food supply chains were pressured by domestic and cross-border disruptions. Restrictions on domestic transport, especially in the first half of 2020, caused immediate, large-scale impacts on entire stages of food supply chains. This restricted access to farm inputs, such as seeds, fertilizers, and crop protection products. Immobile urban transport meant that high-value perishable foods such as fruits and vegetables suffered from limited last-mile delivery to distribution centers and consumers. Many farm activities that entail timely seasonal harvests led to delays and losses in yields and output. Internationally, exports bans aside from cross-border transport restrictions hindered distribution of staple foods, especially for countries that rely on imports. Cambodia and Viet Nam imposed export bans on rice in early 2020, while Myanmar suspended the issuance of export licenses in the same year.[4] The Russian Federation and Ukraine, the world's top wheat producers, banned exports of wheat products.

Indicators also show that the global supply chains were significantly tested and disrupted during the pandemic. Monthly data from the Federal Reserve Bank of New York's Global Supply Chain Pressure Index, which integrates transportation cost data and manufacturing indicators, show these trends, with the index peaking in early 2022 before declining to its historical average level (Figure 14). A key reason for the second round of pressures was disruption to container shipping, due in part to pandemic-related port lockdowns, but also productivity constraints in some countries. The index reflects that at the worst of the supply chain crisis, over 10% of the world's container carrying capacity was onboard vessels waiting at seaports to be unloaded. The figure consistently shows that a rise in supply chain pressure occurred following increased waiting times for container ships at ports and related shipping costs. This highlights the importance of both trade and transport facilitation in addressing supply chain resilience.

---

[4] Effective 1 February 2021, ADB placed a temporary hold on sovereign project disbursements and new contracts in Myanmar.

Figure 14: **Global Supply Chain Pressure Index and Related Indicators during the Pandemic, 2019–2022**

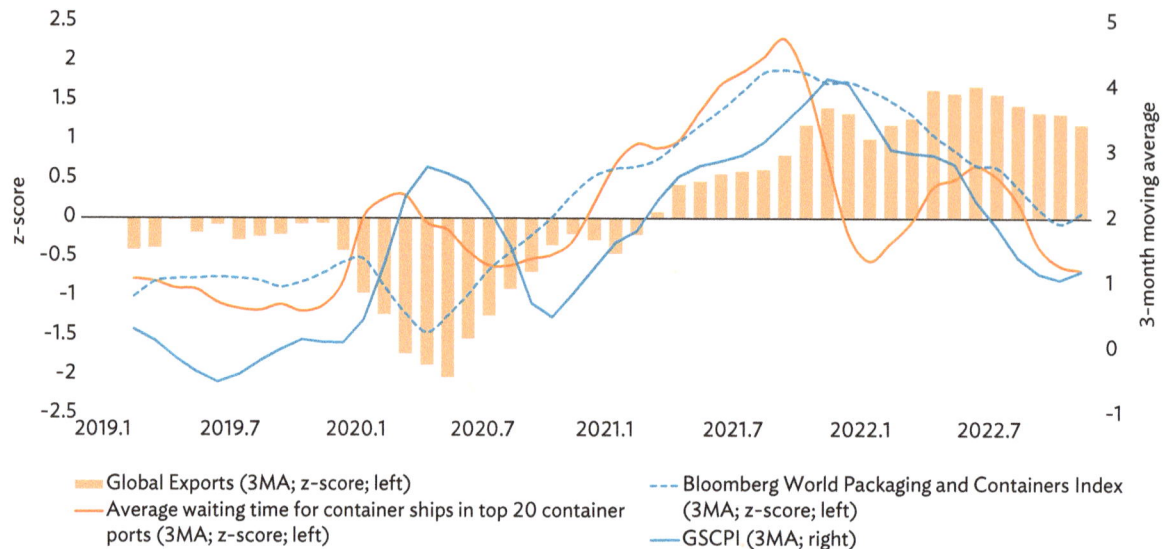

- Global Exports (3MA; z-score; left)
- Average waiting time for container ships in top 20 container ports (3MA; z-score; left)
- Bloomberg World Packaging and Containers Index (3MA; z-score; left)
- GSCPI (3MA; right)

3MA = 3-month moving average, GSCPI = global supply chain pressure index.

Note: The indexes have been normalized using z-scores. Calculated mean and standard deviation of the indexes were for January 2018 to 23 December 2022.

Sources: Federal Reserve Bank of New York GSCPI Database https://www.newyorkfed.org/research/policy/gscpi ; Bloomberg; UN Commodity Trade Statistics Database https://comtradeplus.un.org/ (all accessed 3 December 2023); and Korea Maritime Institute.

4.2 | Factors Affecting GVC Resilience

Measuring resilience in GVCs is complex. This is due to the multifaceted nature of elements such as supply, demand, logistics, market dynamics, differences across industries and regions, as well as the difficulties in securing precise data. Additionally, the lack of standardized interpretation of resilience adds to the challenge. Consequently, much of the current discussion centers on identifying and understanding key factors that contribute to resilience in GVCs. This section discusses these determinants, drawing from insights from recent and widely referenced empirical research and meta-analyses.

4.2.1 Supply chain visibility, transparency, and role of technology

Various studies provide insights into the factors that enhance supply chain visibility, which facilitates quicker adaptation and response to unforeseen challenges. Kalaiarasan et al. (2022) for instance conducted a systematic literature review of empirical research on supply chain visibility. They proposed frameworks for understanding supply chain visibility, encompassing four key elements: antecedents (or prerequisites), barriers and challenges, drivers, and effects (resilience as part of the effects). The foundations of supply chain visibility are reflected in the antecedents, where an integrated supply chain (process) can be achieved through collaboration (people), aided by technology. Barriers and challenges are factors that hinder the improvement of supply chain visibility like costs, privacy concerns of customers, and independent thinking of supply chain players. Compliance requirements of the industry or customers, and responsible sourcing are among the drivers for better supply chain visibility. Other important drivers also include risk management and the demands for sustainability. Ultimately, improved supply chain visibility leads to higher capability of supply chain players, which will subsequently result in higher performance via economic, social, and environmental sustainability (Figure 15).

Examining the electrical and electronics sector in Malaysia, Mubarik et al. (2021) used survey data from 154 firms and applied structural equation modeling to examine supply chain visibility. They found that supply chain mapping, which involves representing network relationships, flows, and dynamics in a simplified yet realistic manner, significantly improves supply chain visibility and, consequently, supply chain resilience. Using the survey based on a number of supply chain exports in industry and academia, Gebhardt et al. (2022) also found that supply chain mapping is one of a prioritized list of future measures to enhance resilience, along with supplier selection and supply chain collaboration (e.g., information and resource sharing with supply chain partners for better risk management).

Technology enhances supply chains by facilitating supply chain visibility. While examining 262 articles on innovative technologies, data analytics, and supply chain resiliency, Iftikhar et al. (2022) provided a comprehensive review in which Industry 4.0 technologies are identified to predict and mitigate supply chain interruption via improved visibility and traceability, citing food and pharmaceutical supply chains (Figure 15).

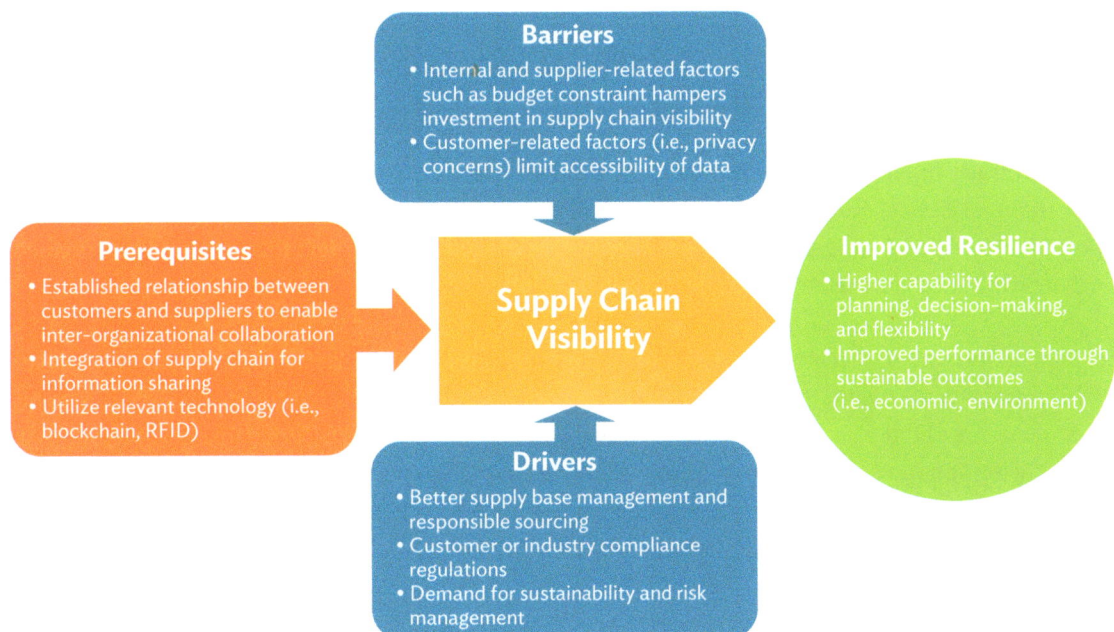

Figure 15: **Framework of Supply Chain Visibility**

Barriers
- Internal and supplier-related factors such as budget constraint hampers investment in supply chain visibility
- Customer-related factors (i.e., privacy concerns) limit accessibility of data

Prerequisites
- Established relationship between customers and suppliers to enable inter-organizational collaboration
- Integration of supply chain for information sharing
- Utilize relevant technology (i.e., blockchain, RFID)

Supply Chain Visibility

Improved Resilience
- Higher capability for planning, decision-making, and flexibility
- Improved performance through sustainable outcomes (i.e., economic, environment)

Drivers
- Better supply base management and responsible sourcing
- Customer or industry compliance regulations
- Demand for sustainability and risk management

RFID = radio-frequency identification.
Source: Authors based on Kalaiarasan et al. (2022).

4.2.2 Diversification

Diversification of suppliers can effectively protect domestic production against country-specific supply shocks. This highlights the role of diversification in bolstering GVC resilience (Schwellnus, Haramboure, and Samek 2023). Similarly, Malacrino, Mohommad, and Presbite (2022) found that countries with a broader range of trade partners experience less adverse impacts from pandemic-induced lockdowns and disruptions in output and growth volatility. However, the approach to address GVC vulnerability stemming from excessive concentration should be balanced, recognizing the costs associated with supply diversification, partial onshoring, and technological substitution (Schwellnus, Haramboure, and Samek 2023). The goal is not to dismantle GVCs but to enhance their resilience through a strategic increase in diversification (IMF 2022).

4.2.3 Logistics

While only a few studies explore the link between logistics and GVCs, the former has traditionally been a critical element in international trade that significantly affects overall trade costs. Gani (2017) found a significant positive correlation between logistics performance and international trade, suggesting that investing in logistics infrastructure can positively impact a country's trade activities. Halaszovich and Kinra (2020) showed that well-developed national transportation systems not only enhance trade but also help in attracting foreign direct investment. Studies emphasize the importance of logistics and transportation systems in the dynamics of GVCs and international trade, particularly highlighting the need for continuous development in logistics to boost economic growth. Memedovic et al. (2008), for instance, argued that advancements in logistics, such as containerization and information technology (IT) integration in distribution, are vital for reaping the benefits of GVCs. They note that developing countries often lag due to less efficient inland transport systems, impacting their resilience to distribution costs.

4.2.4 Others: Access to finance, political and economic stability, regulatory compliance and standards

The lens of trade finance, a crucial facilitator of cross-border trade, reveals additional factors influencing supply chain resilience. ADB's Trade Finance Gap, Growth, and Jobs Survey 2023 (ADB 2023), which gathered insights from banks and firms, explored the repercussions of significant barriers to accessing trade finance, such as high interest rates and the impact of the Russian invasion of Ukraine.

According to the survey, macrofinancial instability can heighten a bank's funding expenses, affecting its profits and the availability of credit (Figure 16). Around 64% of banks identified the tightening of credit due to high interest rates as a primary obstacle in providing trade finance. Additionally, 61% of banks pointed out that geopolitical tensions and post-pandemic macroeconomic stressors influence financiers' risk appetite, potentially restricting trade financing access, particularly in emerging markets. These elements could exacerbate the trade finance gap, increasing the vulnerability of supply chains.

While digitalization is often touted for its role in reducing trade costs, the survey notes that the high expense of digital transformation stands as the main hurdle in digitizing banking operations to support trade (Figure 17). Challenges also include understanding and implementing technology, the absence of globally recognized laws and standards and discrepancy in recognizing electronic trade documents across countries, and the inadequate interoperability of existing platforms, all contributing to escalated costs.

Figure 16:   Barriers Financial Institutions Face in Servicing Trade Finance (% of bank responses)

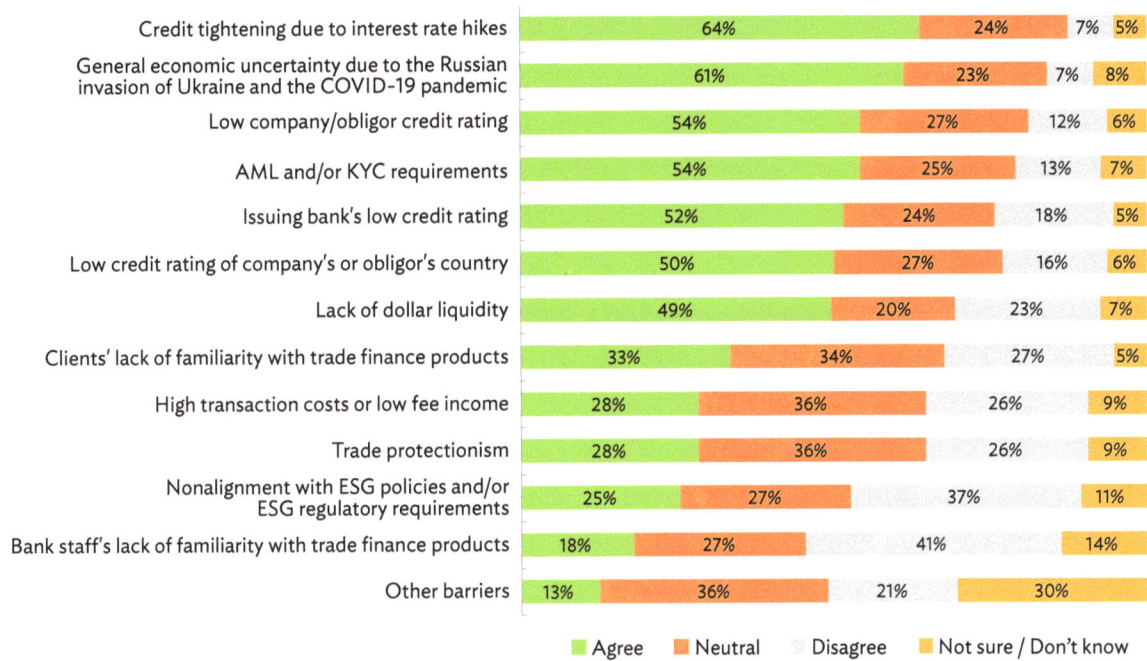

Barrier	Agree	Neutral	Disagree	Not sure / Don't know
Credit tightening due to interest rate hikes	64%	24%	7%	5%
General economic uncertainty due to the Russian invasion of Ukraine and the COVID-19 pandemic	61%	23%	7%	8%
Low company/obligor credit rating	54%	27%	12%	6%
AML and/or KYC requirements	54%	25%	13%	7%
Issuing bank's low credit rating	52%	24%	18%	5%
Low credit rating of company's or obligor's country	50%	27%	16%	6%
Lack of dollar liquidity	49%	20%	23%	7%
Clients' lack of familiarity with trade finance products	33%	34%	27%	5%
High transaction costs or low fee income	28%	36%	26%	9%
Trade protectionism	28%	36%	26%	9%
Nonalignment with ESG policies and/or ESG regulatory requirements	25%	27%	37%	11%
Bank staff's lack of familiarity with trade finance products	18%	27%	41%	14%
Other barriers	13%	36%	21%	30%

AML = anti-money laundering, COVID-19 = coronavirus disease, ESG = environmental, social, and governance, KYC = know your customer.
Source: ADB. (2023).

Figure 17:   Barriers to Digitalizing Banks' Business and Trade Portfolio (% of bank responses)

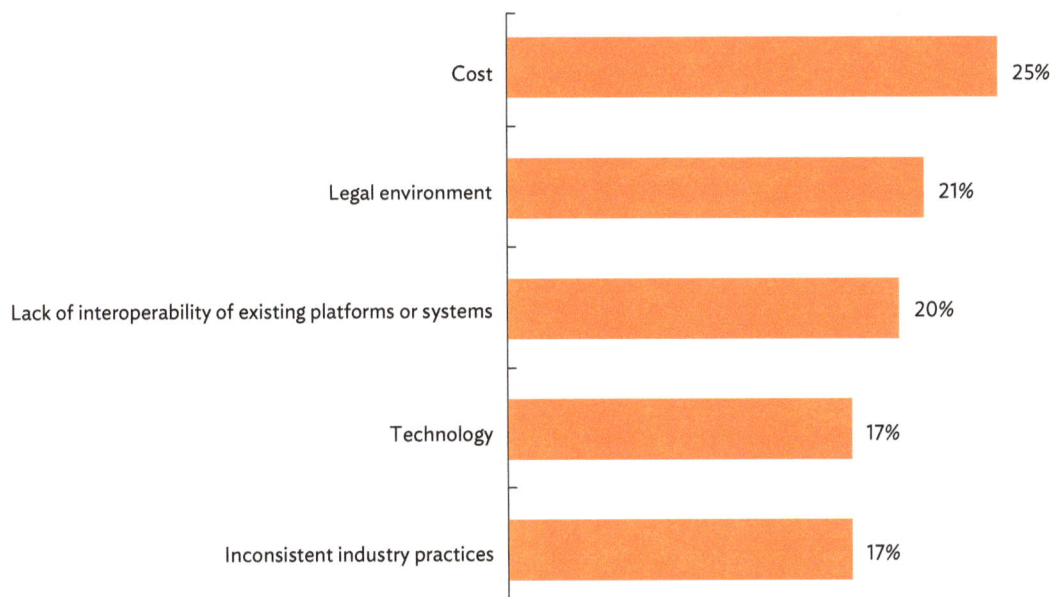

Barrier	%
Cost	25%
Legal environment	21%
Lack of interoperability of existing platforms or systems	20%
Technology	17%
Inconsistent industry practices	17%

Source: ADB. (2023).

5 Trade Facilitation for Sustainability and Resilience in GVCs

Building on the discussion of trade facilitation impacts on GVC participation and factors affecting sustainability and resilience in GVCs, this section provides an analytical framework to bring these elements together.

5.1 | Framework on GVC Sustainability and Resilience and Trade Facilitation

Enhancing GVC resilience is a multifaceted endeavor, and sustainability is a core driver of resilience in GVCs. As outlined earlier, GVC resilience involves diversification of suppliers and markets, increased supply chain visibility and transparency, flexibility of production and logistics systems, and adoption of advanced technologies. Adherence to regulatory compliance and standards, coupled with financial strength and flexibility, are also fundamental (Figure 18). Moreover, by prioritizing sustainability, GVCs can effectively mitigate risks associated with environmental changes, maintain compliance with global regulations, and prevent operational disruptions. Sustainable practices enhance resource efficiency and reduce costs, making GVCs more adaptable to fluctuations in resources. A focus on sustainability also attracts investors who prioritize environmental, social, and governance (ESG) criteria, which is essential for growth and resilience in a competitive global market.

5.1.1 Trade facilitation measures are instrumental in enhancing sustainability within GVCs.

By improving supply chain transparency and traceability, trade facilitation measures not only increase the predictability and speed of goods movement but also help companies sustainably source materials and efficiently allocate resources.[5] Further, adherence to standards in behind-the-border and at-the-border environments, including Sanitary and Phytosanitary standards, contributes to GVC sustainability.

---

[5] Trade facilitation aims primarily to enhance trade by reducing trade costs. The discussion here focuses on trade facilitation measures that directly help mitigate the impact of climate change. The direct effects include the environmental benefits of efficient trade facilitation, such as the reduction in paper use due to trade digitalization and the savings in time and costs resulting from decreased waiting times. Indirect effects, meanwhile, link trade facilitation to climate change through trade mechanisms that may not necessarily mitigate greenhouse gas emissions (see Box 2 for discussion on trade facilitation and environmental sustainability).

Figure 18: Factors Affecting GVC Resilience and Sustainability, and Trade Facilitation-Related Factors

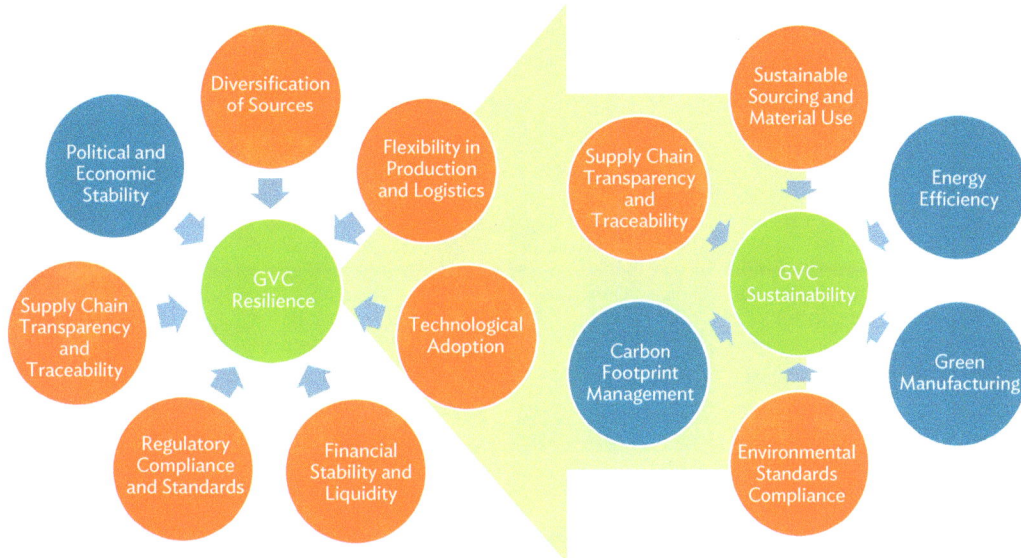

GVC = global value chain.
Note: Orange circles represent factors with high relevance to trade facilitation.
Source: Authors.

As global awareness and action on climate change intensify, trade-related measures are increasingly being used as a strategic tool to address environmental challenges. This trend is evident from the significant rise in environmental-related notifications to the WTO. From 2009, environmental-related notifications to the WTO have increased by 61%, growing from 480 notifications in 2009 to 775 notifications in 2022 (Figure 19). Most of these environment-related notifications were pursued under the WTO Agreement on Technical Barriers to Trade,[6] and the Agreement on Sanitary and Phytosanitary Measures, highlighting their importance and potential to support climate mitigation and adaptation.

The imperative to limit carbon dioxide (CO_2) emissions in economic activity makes it even more important for countries to adopt ambitious trade facilitation reforms. This entails moving toward full implementation of the WTO Trade Facilitation Agreement, and preferably exceeding that benchmark. While decarbonization policies might increase trade costs—including transport costs from higher prices of renewables—and pressure GVC linkages, scope exists for improved trade facilitation to act in the opposite direction. Implementing such policies can help ensure that GVCs remain as widespread as possible, even if trade costs linked to decarbonization policies increase substantially.

---

[6]   One example is Viet Nam's Circular on Energy Efficiency Labeling Rules for Electric Vehicles and Motorcycles (Government of Viet Nam, Ministry of Transport 2022) that mandates an energy labelling scheme for electric or hybrid vehicles to help consumers make environment-conscious decisions. The label contains information on fuel consumption and carbon emissions associated with using the product.

Figure 19: **Number of Environment-Related Notifications by WTO Agreement, 2009–2022**

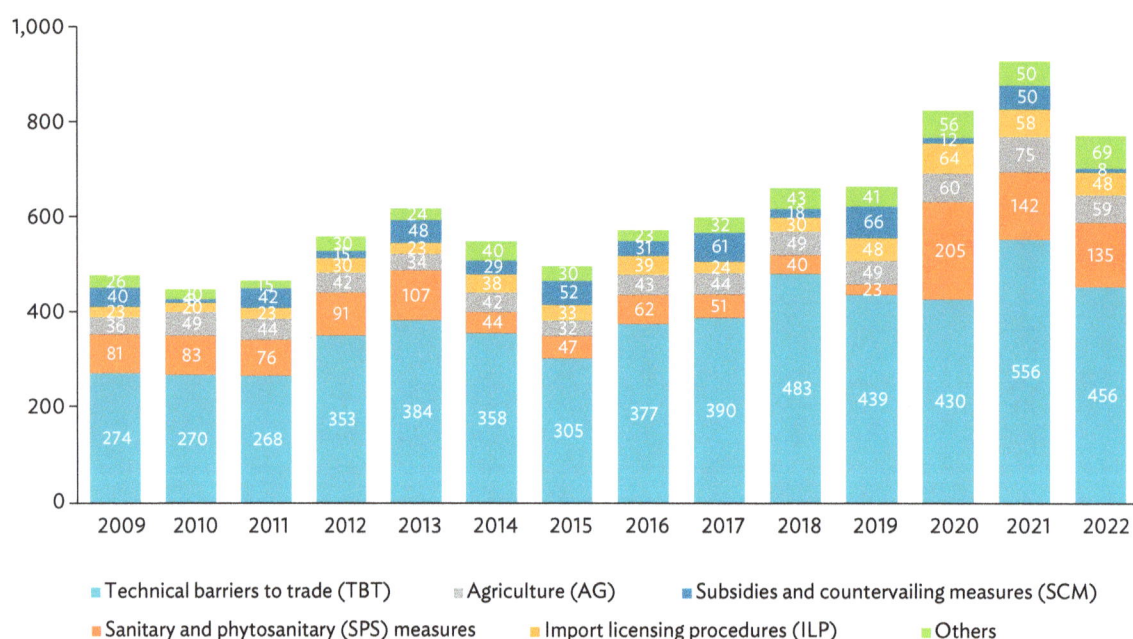

WTO = World Trade Organization.

Note: Others include quantitative restrictions, trade facilitation, regional trade agreements, government procurement, trade-related aspects of intellectual property rights, General Agreement on Trade in Services, state trading, safeguards, customs valuation, trade-related investment measures, anti-dumping, other notification provisions, balance of payments, pre-shipment inspection, and rules of origin.

Source: WTO. Environmental Database. https://edb.wto.org/notifications (accessed 15 December 2023).

Moreover, the transition to renewable energy sources requires international trade in technology. Products like solar cells, batteries, and wind turbines are not manufactured in all countries. Facilitating their movement across borders is an important way of ensuring environmentally friendly goods are widely available across the region. GVC development in environmental sectors can be an important part of ensuring that trade takes place in an efficient way. Trade facilitation has a role to play by lowering trade costs, in tandem with efforts to reduce tariff barriers.

5.1.2 Trade facilitation measures also help to reinforce GVC resilience.

Improved customs procedures and enhanced cross-border information sharing heighten transparency, suggesting that more sustainable GVC practices can lead to increased resilience through clearer trade processes. Trade facilitation also enables firms to more easily access international partnerships and contributes to logistics and supply management agility via simplified procedures and faster border crossings. This, coupled with the promotion of paperless trade, supports the uninterrupted flow of data and goods across borders. Harmonizing standards and regulations simplifies compliance, and facilitating easier access to trade finance strengthens the financial stability of businesses within GVCs.

Trade facilitation policies play a crucial role in enabling firms to swiftly move goods and source from alternative suppliers with minimal additional costs. Although these policies might not directly determine the structures of GVCs or specific risk management practices, their significant impact on altering business dynamics is key to enhancing GVC resilience. This becomes particularly important in risk management for businesses in GVCs. Emphasizing technologies and transparency for risk identification and management, creating supply chain redundancies, and developing capabilities for rapid response are essential components of this strategy (Lund et al. 2020).

The increasing complexity of supply chains in GVCs necessitates the adoption of digital technologies for efficient trade facilitation. GVCs in many sectors are highly complex, involving hundreds or even thousands of suppliers—including small and medium-sized enterprises (SMEs)—spread across a range of countries. Technology is not only vital to manage risk and deal with unforeseen shocks, but also to ensure the smooth day-to-day operation of the supply chain in "typical" circumstances, in particular the timely delivery of goods. Firms of all sizes need access to real-time information on shipment progress and delay sources. So the extent to which border agencies use compatible and interoperable technology solutions and make that kind of information available to shippers, will be increasingly important in light of the heightened importance of risk management in the post-COVID-19 era.

Table 2 summarizes these sustainability and resilience factors and the role of trade facilitation, along with examples of trade facilitation measures that support each factor.

Table 2: Factors Affecting GVC Resilience and Relevance to Trade Facilitation

Factors	Description	Role of Trade Facilitation	Examples of Trade Facilitation Initiatives/ Measures
GVC Sustainability			
Supply Chain Transparency and Traceability	Tracking the transformation of a product from raw material to finished good.	Enhance transparency and flow of cross-border information exchange on supply chain events.	Traceability for Sustainable Trade: A Framework to design Traceability Systems for Cross Border Trade.
Sustainable Sourcing and Material Use	Relying on suppliers that have sustainable practices and demonstrate environmental protection in their operations.	Allow better access to production inputs that are sustainably sourced.	Streamlined border controls and simplified procedures for inputs and materials that are sustainably sourced; UNECE Sustainable Procurement.
Environmental Standards Compliance	System designed to protect the environment through laws and regulations.	Ensure environmental sustainability and prevention of illegal trade, environmentally destructive commodities, and substances like hazardous waste and endangered species.	Green Customs Initiative; WTO Agreement on Fisheries Subsidies.

continued next page

Table 2: *Continued*

Factors	Description	Role of Trade Facilitation	Examples of Trade Facilitation Initiatives/ Measures
GVC Resilience			
Supply Chain Visibility and Transparency	Knowing where inputs come from and where products are going through advanced tracking can identify potential disruption points	Enhances transparency through improved customs procedures and better information sharing across borders.	APEC List of Environmental Goods; WCO's HS classification for COVID-19 medical supplies; ADB's Supply Chain Maps for Pandemic-Fighting Products
Diversification	Relying on a few suppliers or markets makes the chain vulnerable to localized disruptions	Helps firms better access and establish relationships with international partners.	Most trade facilitation measures help reduce trade costs, leading to enhanced export diversification
Flexible Production and Logistics	The ability to quickly alter production processes and logistics in response to changing conditions	Supports the agility needed in logistics and supply management through simplified procedures and faster border crossings.	Authorized operators (specified in WTO TFA)
Technological Adoption	Improving efficiency and providing real-time data for better decision-making through the use of advanced technologies	Paperless trade facilitation supports the seamless flow of data and goods across borders	UN Framework Agreement on Facilitation of Cross-Border Paperless Trade in Asia and the Pacific
Regulatory Compliance and Standards	Adherence to international standards and regulatory compliance ensures smooth cross-border operations	Making compliance easier by harmonizing standards and regulations.	ICC Digital Standards Initiative; ISSB Sustainability Disclosure standards; UNCITRAL Model Law on Electronic Transferable Records
Financial Strength and Flexibility	The financial robustness of companies in the value chain impacts resilience	Easier access to trade finance can support the financial stability of businesses in GVCs.	G20 support for trade finance; national and regional trade finance measures

APEC = Asia-Pacific Economic Cooperation, GVC = global value chain, HS = Harmonized System, ICC = International Chamber of Commerce, ISSB = International Sustainable Standards Board, TFA = trade facilitation agreement, UNECE = United Nations Economic Commission for Europe, UNCITRAL = United Nations Commission on International Trade Law, WCO = World Customs Organization, WTO = World Trade Organization.

Source: Authors.

Box 2: Trade Facilitation and Environmental Sustainability

The relationship between trade facilitation and climate change is inconspicuous, which may partly explain why this topic is not sufficiently explored. A paper by Kim, Basu-Das, and Ardaniel (2024) discusses the transmission channel through which trade facilitation can impact climate change, featuring direct and indirect linkages. Direct effect refers to climate change consequences of trade facilitation measures like reduction in paper usage from trade digitalization and time/costs savings of reduced waiting time. Indirect effect connects trade facilitation to climate change via trade. Trade facilitation, by increasing trade, can also be environmentally negative if scale and composition effects dominate the technique effect (Tamiotti et al. 2009). Trade facilitation can also indirectly increase export diversification and global value chain (GVC) participation, which could in turn increase carbon dioxide (CO_2) emissions.

The table summarizes the literature on how trade facilitation can promote environmental sustainability from the direct impact perspective. For example, by facilitating trade through the implementation of single window, carbon emissions were reduced for Vanuatu and Timor-Leste, while better management of legal trade of wildlife is seen in Sri Lanka. Paperless trade can also save at least 8,969 metric tons of carbon dioxide equivalent (CO_2e) for Bangladesh, an average of 13.8 million tons of CO_2e for Asia and the Pacific, and 36.1 million tons of CO_2e when it is carried out globally. Notably, however, most measures implemented for trade facilitation that can improve environmental quality are narrow in scope, and limited only to border-related activities. This may be because trade facilitation measures are to a great extent associated with the automation of customs procedures.

Empirical Evidence of Trade Facilitation Contributing to Environmental Quality

Study	Type of Trade Facilitation Activities	Target Measures	Findings	Study Setting
Ibrahim and Ajide (2022)	Six components of trade facilitation (including costs, and the documents and time required for trade)	Emissions of CO_2 and N_2O	A significant negative relationship between trade facilitation and environmental pollution	48 African countries
Musyoki (2020)	Trade information portal for Kenya's trade procedures	Number of documents eliminated	The trade information portal was able to eliminate 64 documents and simplify 40 trade procedures since its launch in 2017	Kenya
Sirimanne and Adhikari (2022)	Electronic Single Window (automation in customs clearance and sanitary and phytosanitary applications)	CO_2	Reduced CO_2 by 5,827 kilograms (kg) through goods clearance processes	Vanuatu
ASYCUDA (2022) and United Nations (2021)	Electronic Single Window	CO_2 and ozone-depleting substances	Reduction of 14,492 kg of CO_2 emissions and better management of ozone-depleting imports	Timor-Leste

continued next page

Box 2: *Continued*

Study	Type of Trade Facilitation Activities	Target Measures	Findings	Study Setting
Dai (2021)	Enabling trade index (market access, border administration, infrastructure, and operating environment)	Trade in environmental goods	A 1% increase in the trade index value resulted in a 3.39% increase in export value of environmental goods and 3.89% in import value of environmental goods.	Viet Nam
ASYCUDA (2020)	Electronic permit system	Management of wildlife trade	Electronic solution helps to prevent illegal trade of endangered species.	Sri Lanka
Duval and Hardy (2021)	Paperless trade	GHG emissions	Implementation of paperless trade can save an average of 13.8 million tons of CO_2 equivalent for Asia, and an estimated 36.1 million tons of CO_2 equivalent for the world.	Asia and the Pacific and World
Natasha, Lim, and Duval (2021)	Paperless trade	GHG emissions	Paperless trade can save 8,969—30, 333 metric tons of CO_2e	Bangladesh
Lucas (2021)	Customs inspection	CO_2	Enhanced efficiency in border procedures can reduce emissions in land border crossings.	US, Mexico, and Canada
Northern American Partnership (2019)	Border clearance for low-risk shipments	CO_2, particulate matters	The Free and Secure Trade Program and Unified Cargo Processing can lead to 85% reduction in emissions.	Nogales-Mariposa border of the US and Mexico

ASYCUDA = Automated System for Customs Data, CO_2 = carbon dioxide, GHG = greenhouse gas emissions, N_2O = Nitrous oxide, US = United States.

Source: Authors.

5.2 | GVC Sustainability and Resilience-Adjusted Trade Facilitation Implementation

The next question pertains to the perception of trade facilitation through the lenses of sustainability and resilience in GVCs. Specifically, how does trade facilitation appear when these two aspects of GVCs are given greater emphasis in each facet of trade facilitation, such as transparency and paperless trade?

In the following exercise, we aim to align specific trade facilitation measures with sustainability and resilience in GVCs, providing an indicative assessment of the potential impact of trade facilitation. Previously, Kim, Basu-Das, and Ardaniel(2024) engaged in a thought experiment, assigning scores to trade facilitation measures based on their perceived impact on greenhouse gas (GHG) reduction. These scores range from low (1) to high (3) and were applied to a subgroup of the UN Global Survey on Digital and Sustainable

Trade Facilitation. Their findings suggest that digital trade facilitation measures significantly mitigate carbon emissions compared to traditional trade facilitation measures, indicating a need for modifications to traditional practices to evolve toward climate-smart trade facilitation.

Building on the determinants of GVC resilience and their relation to trade facilitation discussed earlier, the approach in Kim, Basu-Das, and Ardaniel (2024) is expanded to include resilience alongside sustainability (Appendix). The average score for each subgroup (comprising nine categories: (i) transparency, (ii) formalities, (iii) institutional arrangement and cooperation, (iv) transit facilitation, (v) paperless trade, (vi) cross-border paperless trade, (vii) trade facilitation for SMEs, (viii) agricultural trade facilitation, and (ix) women in trade facilitation) is recalculated for each country, applying the perceived degree of sustainability and resilience relevance as weights to trade facilitation.

Figure 20 illustrates levels of trade facilitation implementation when sustainability and resilience in GVCs are more prominently considered, broken down by subregion. The results, assuming a base implementation rate of 100 in 2023, show varying discrepancies between the original and adjusted scores across subregions. For instance, trade facilitation measures in Southeast Asia lean more toward green practices, such as the use of digital tools including single windows, which also bolster GVC resilience. However, the findings imply that trade facilitation measures in the Pacific may be less adept at responding to GVC disruptions. While this is a preliminary exercise based on assumed, indicative associations, it suggests that trade facilitation focus should evolve to meet the increasing demands for quick responses to supply chain disruptions and the reduction of environmental impacts.

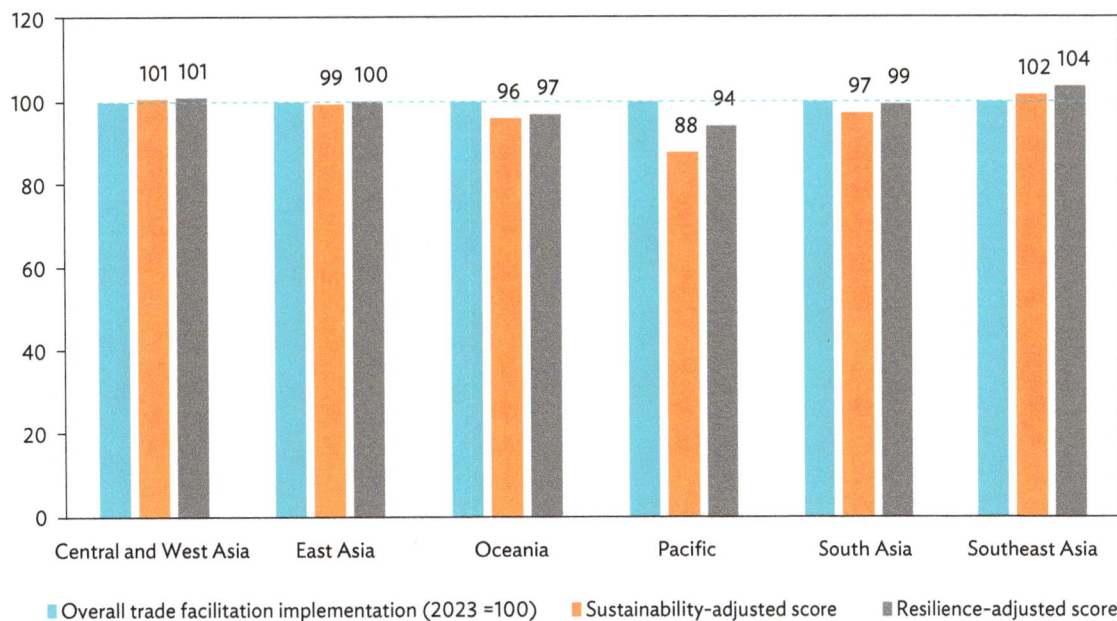

Figure 20: **Level of Trade Facilitation Implementation with Adjustment for Sustainability and Resilience in Global Value Chains** (2023 = 100)

Legend: ■ Overall trade facilitation implementation (2023 =100)   ■ Sustainability-adjusted score   ■ Resilience-adjusted score

Source: UN Global Survey on Digital and Sustainable Trade Facilitation. untfsurvey.org; Authors based on Kim, Basu-Das, and Ardaniel (2024).

6 Conclusions and Policy Implications

Trade facilitation has been an important determinant of the region's economic success, in tandem with efforts to lower tariff barriers. All countries in the region have a clear interest in ambitiously scheduling and implementing commitments under the World Trade Organization (WTO) Trade Facilitation Agreement (TFA). Similarly, regional experience suggests that broader efforts to reduce trade costs, including through digitalization and transport facilitation, can bear fruit through increased support for global value chain (GVC) expansion.

An important takeaway for policymakers is that the WTO TFA should be seen as a benchmark, not an objective. It represents a globally agreed set of minimum standards, not the frontier of best practice. As such, it is important for economies with performance difficulties—the Pacific island countries, South Asian countries, and landlocked countries—to nonetheless be as ambitious as possible in scheduling commitments. Similarly, economies and multilateral agencies offering technical assistance and capacity building need to prioritize full implementation of the TFA. For those that already have a strong performance base, moving into frontier areas, such as paperless trade and system interoperability, is a way to continue to reduce trade costs and remain attractive to GVCs.

Although advancing trade facilitation is a general priority for the region, the salience of different measures varies by subregion and country. The Trade Facilitation Index of the Organisation for Economic Co-operation and Development (OECD) suggests that external and internal cooperation, as well as automation, are areas in which at least some subregions see particular issues. The digital and sustainable trade facilitation data, on the other hand, highlight gender, small and medium-sized enterprises (SMEs), and cross-border paperless trade as areas where most subregions display performance deficits. Overall, the most effort is required in the Pacific and South Asia, where trade facilitation performance lags relative to other subregions. Yet, improvement is evident in all regions. The existence of world leader economies in trade facilitation, for instance in Oceania and East Asia, indicates substantial scope for experience sharing and learning from successful reforms in Asia and the Pacific.

While Asia and the Pacific has benefited greatly from GVC development over recent decades, the current international environment poses a mix of challenges and opportunities. On the one hand, environmental policy is moving higher up the agenda, particularly as it relates to climate change. This new salience means that demand for goods will to some extent shift in directions like electric vehicles (EVs) and renewable energy products. These products can be, and indeed already are, manufactured through GVCs, including in Asia and the Pacific. So there are commercial opportunities in these areas that policymakers should facilitate by ensuring that the trade policy environment is as conducive as possible to free movement of environmental goods and services across borders.

At the same time, however, decarbonization will likely pose challenges for GVC development, primarily through a cost channel. GVCs are engineered to minimize cost along the supply chain. But tackling climate change involves either explicitly or implicitly imposing prices on carbon, which will likely increase the cost profile of carbon-intensive sectors. While businesses and policymakers need to be alive to this issue, existing evidence suggests that it is unlikely to have major impacts on GVC development and operation in a general sense. While there could be stresses and disruptions at a micro level, there is little in aggregate data to suggest that GVC development as a whole needs to be retooled or rethought as a result of the climate challenge. A key question, however, relates to the extent to which policy should be involved in these processes. As yet, there is no strong evidence of the types of market failure that would motivate a strong policy intervention. A first step could be the introduction of transparency mechanisms that facilitate information flow between businesses and governments, in particular in supply chains deemed critical.

Looking ahead, it is imperative to adopt digitalization in trade facilitation to enhance GVC resilience and sustainability. The emergence of challenges in GVCs, particularly those highlighted by the COVID-19 pandemic, underscores the need for this role. This calls for accelerating the adoption of the Framework Agreement on Facilitation of Cross-Border Paperless Trade in Asia and the Pacific as well as bilateral and regional digital economy agreements that promote liberalized rules on data flows, electronic transactions, and digital trade facilitation. The ASEAN Agreement on Electronic Commerce for instance provides a set of policies and rules to govern cross-border e-commerce in the subregion and includes facilitating paperless trading and electronic authentication, while the digital economy agreement between Singapore and Australia builds on their existing trade agreement by supplementing it with cooperation on e-invoicing, e-certification for agricultural exports and imports, and trade facilitation. Emerging technologies such as big data and analytics, the Internet of Things, blockchain, and others are already in use in tracking supply chains. Continuous support for developing countries is vital in achieving a digitalized trading environment to ensure inclusive, resilient, and sustainable evolution.

Environmental sustainability is indeed becoming increasingly important in recent trade agreements, reflecting a global shift toward integrating environmental considerations into international trade policies. For instance, several trade agreements, including the Comprehensive and Progressive Agreement for Trans-Pacific Partnership, which entered into force in December 2018, highlight the need to align trade policies with environmental protection and Sustainable Development Goals. The Singapore-Australia Green Economy Agreement, which was signed in October 2022, focuses on promoting green innovations and environmental services. Similarly, the UK-New Zealand Free Trade Agreement (FTA) places a strong emphasis on trade of environmental goods and services, highlighting this as a key area of collaboration. Furthermore, the Agreement on Climate Change, Trade, and Sustainability, involving New Zealand, Costa Rica, Fiji, Iceland, Norway, and Switzerland, is an ongoing effort to create a comprehensive framework linking climate change, trade, and sustainable development. These agreements signify a growing recognition of the need to balance economic growth with environmental stewardship, ensuring that trade policies support and enhance global sustainability goals.

The emergence of green trade facilitation in international trade underscores the need to integrate environmental sustainability into the trade facilitation framework. Green trade facilitation highlights the importance of embracing digital transformation to reduce carbon emissions; promoting climate-smart transport; enhancing green customs initiatives; and integrating environmental, social, and governance (ESG) considerations into trade finance (Box 3). Additionally, the implementation of advanced electronic permitting systems and support for circular economy practices are also important. However, there is a pressing need to clarify and standardize the scope of green trade facilitation to ensure uniformity in its application and effectiveness globally. Such clarification will guide policymakers, industry stakeholders, and international bodies in their concerted efforts to align trade processes with Sustainable Development Goals.

By prioritizing transport infrastructure that aligns with environmental goals, the transport sector can play a pivotal role in fostering a more sustainable global trade. Addressing emissions from international transportation is crucial due to its integral role in trade. According to the International Transport Forum (ITF 2021), transport activity is expected to more than double by 2050, with freight transport increasing by 2.6 times. CO_2 emissions from transport could increase by 16% within the same time frame. Even with current commitments to decarbonization, the increase in demand is likely to offset any emissions reductions, highlighting the urgent need for more robust decarbonization policies in this sector. Investment in sustainable transport infrastructure is critical to support eco-friendly goods movement within GVCs. This includes developing efficient transport networks, leveraging renewable energy sources, and enhancing logistics systems to minimize environmental impact. Such investments not only contribute to reducing emissions, but also ensure long-term economic viability and resilience in global trade networks.

Enhancing institutional quality in trade facilitation at the national and regional levels plays a crucial role in sustainable and resilient GVC development. Measures like the establishment of national trade facilitation committees and improved border agency cooperation significantly contribute to efficient trade, fostering GVC resilience and sustainability. These initiatives, particularly when paired with regional cooperation efforts, lead to a more integrated and robust trade environment. A comprehensive approach that combines internal governance improvements with regional collaboration is essential for sustainable and resilient GVC development in the rapidly changing global economic landscape.

Building sustainable and resilient global supply chains hinges on cultivating deeper cooperation. Trade agreements in Asia are becoming broader as well as more modern and digital in scope. As a response to disruptions induced by the pandemic, the Comprehensive and Progressive Agreement on Trans-Pacific Partnership has initiated a review of its provisions to include strengthening supply chain resilience to withstand external shocks and disruptions, while the Indo-Pacific Economic Framework for Prosperity also includes resilient supply chains in its focus (Jacobi 2024). In addition, the significance of fostering sustainable and resilient global supply chains was included in the discussions of the 28th Conference of the Parties (COP28) in December 2023. Diversifying supply chains, use of advance technology in supply chains, and sourcing responsibly are among the recommended measures in developing supply chain resilience and sustainability (Al Zeyoudi et al. 2023). This requires closer coordination among governments, the private sector including industry chambers, the many small businesses involved in supply chains, and other stakeholders. Further deepening trading relationships and greater global cooperation will bind trading partners, which may help mitigate disruptions. There should also be access to accurate data and information to guide decisions in a timely manner.

Box 3: Scope of Green Trade Facilitation

The concept of "green trade facilitation," while not rigorously defined, is generally understood to encompass more than just reducing trade barriers. It integrates environmental considerations into the core of international trade, which includes use of digital technologies for efficiency, promotion of environmentally sustainable practices, enforcement of environmental laws, and fostering green trade innovation. Areas of green trade facilitation can include

- **Digitalization for climate-smart trade and transport facilitation:** Emphasizing the need for fully digital end-to-end trade transactions, which can significantly reduce greenhouse gas emissions. For instance, in the Asia and Pacific region, fully digitalizing each trade transaction using tools like ASYHUB, which visualizes maritime end-to-end supply chains, along with single windows, could save about 13 million tons of carbon dioxide (CO_2) annually.[a] The transition toward climate-smart transport is also recommended, since CO_2 emissions from freight transport in the region accounted for 42% of all transport-related CO_2 in 2019.

- **Environmental, social, and governance (ESG) considerations in trade:** Facilitating compliance with ESG requirements for exporters and importers in their trade finance applications and reducing the related costs of compliance, particularly for small and medium-sized enterprises.

- **Digital traceability in supply chain management:** The Cross Industry Supply Chain Track & Trace (T&T), a project of the United Nations Centre for Trade Facilitation and Electronic Business (UN/CEFACT), supports ESG goals, focusing on enhancing supply chain visibility at all stages using standardized electronic data, catering to the growing needs of stakeholders and regulatory requirements, including those for environmental impact and climate change mitigation.

- **Green Customs Initiative:** Implementing trade facilitation measures for environmentally friendly goods and generating environmental benefits through digitalization and paperless procedures. For example, the World Customs Organization established the Asia-Pacific Plastic Waste Project to improve understanding of the Basel Convention's plastic waste requirements and to facilitate legal plastic waste trade using single window approaches.

- **Digital innovation for sustainable trade:** Shifting from paper-based documentation to digitalized processes in customs and trade facilitation, reducing the environmental impact of cross-border trade. In the Kyrgyz Republic, the transition from paper-based documentation to digital certificates of conformity and the implementation of the e-Queue Management System at the Kyrgyz Republic–Uzbekistan border highlight the importance of digital trade facilitation, emphasizing the need for coordination, governance, and tailored IT solutions across borders.

- **Electronic permitting systems:** Implementing digital systems like e-CITES (for endangered species trade) and ePhyto (for plants and plant products), enhancing the efficiency and traceability of trade while supporting environmental conservation. This is proven by the case study of Sri Lanka: implementing the e-CITES system in their Automated System for Customs Data (ASYCUDA) program boosted permit approvals by 40%. Also, average permit processing time dropped significantly, from 175 hours to 36 hours.

continued next page

Box 3: *Continued*

- **Advancing the circular economy:** Promoting trade in secondhand goods, goods for refurbishment, waste, and secondary raw materials to support circular economy practices. The Association of Southeast Asian Nation's (ASEAN) Framework for Circular Economy for the ASEAN Economic Community provides a structured pathway to adopt a circular economy,[b] thereby aligning with the ASEAN sustainability agenda. With the 2013 "e-Basel standards," UN/CEFACT proposed interoperability between borders for waste disposal, non-waste transport data exchanges, and a wide range of IT solutions and knowledge sharing. The standards also cover the notification, consent, and movement of all documentation.

---

[a] ASYHUB is an open, standardized, platform for processing and integrating data between customs information systems, such as ASYCUDAWorld, and other external systems.

[b] See ASEAN (2021) for information.

Source: Authors based on the discussion during the workshop on Emerging Developments and Opportunities in Green Trade Facilitation (3–4 October 2023), co-organized by the Asian Development Bank and the Economic and Social Commission for Asia and the Pacific in collaboration with International Trade Centre and Regional Organizations Cooperation Mechanism for Trade Facilitation partners, together with the United Nations Economic Commission for Europe as part of the 41st UN/CEFACT Forum week held in Bangkok.

Appendix: Possible Impact of Trade Facilitation on Sustainability and Resilience in GVC (Scoring)

Group	Subgroup	Measure	SUSTAINABILITY: Impact on Mitigating GHG Emissions Low-1/ Mid-2/ High-3	Possible Channel	RESILIENCE: Impact on Enhancing GVC Resilience Low-1/ Mid-2/ High-3	Possible Channel
General Trade Facilitation	Transparency	Publication of existing import–export regulations on the internet	3	Lesser trips required to comply with requirements; Reduction in paper use	3	Transparency and availability of trade regulations online increase the visibility and traceability within GVCs, enabling better risk management and adaptability to disruptions.
		Stakeholders' consultation on new draft regulations (before their finalization)	1	Allow for continuous sharing of information in trade facilitation projects.		
		Advance publication/ notification of new trade-related regulations before their implementation (e.g., 30 days prior)	3	Lesser trips required to comply with requirements; Reduction in paper use		
		Advance ruling on tariff classification and origin of imported goods	2	Speeds up clearances and thus reduce waiting time		
		Independent appeal mechanism (for traders to appeal customs rulings and the rulings of other relevant trade control agencies)	1	Unbalance discretionary power of customs may contribute to delay in the release of goods.		
	Formalities	Risk management (for deciding whether a shipment will be physically inspected)	1	May speed up movement of shipments.	2	Streamlining formalities can reduce bottlenecks and enhance the flow of information and goods, which is critical during disruptions.
		Pre-arrival processing	3	Reduction in time spent at the border.		
		Post-clearance audits	1	Improve trader's compliance and facilitate clearance procedures.		
		Separation of release from final determination of customs duties, taxes, fees, and charges	2	Reduction in time spent at the border.		

continued next page

Table: *Continued*

Group	Subgroup	Measure	SUSTAINABILITY: Impact on Mitigating GHG Emissions		RESILIENCE: Impact on Enhancing GVC Resilience	
			Low-1/ Mid-2/ High-3	Possible Channel	Low-1/ Mid-2/ High-3	Possible Channel
General Trade Facilitation	Formalities	Establishment and publication of average release times	1	Lengthy release times will advocate for reducing border delays	2	Streamlining formalities can reduce bottlenecks and enhance the flow of information and goods, which is critical during disruptions.
		Trade facilitation measures for authorized operators	3	Allow qualified operators to benefit from preferential measures like rapid release times, fewer physical inspections, and reduced documentary requirements		
		Expedited shipments	3	Reduce waiting time		
		Acceptance of copies of original supporting documents required for import, export, or transit formalities	2	Reduce waiting time		
	Institutional arrangement and cooperation	Establishment of a National Trade Facilitation Committee or similar body	1	Ensures coordination of various stakeholders for seamless implementation of trade facilitation	3	Enhanced cooperation among border agencies facilitates quicker response times and recovery from disruptions, fostering resilience.
		National legislative framework and/ or institutional arrangements for border agencies cooperation	2	Provides avenue to expedite crossing of shipments and therefore reduce waiting time		
		Government agencies delegating border controls to customs authorities	2	Provides avenue to expedite crossing of shipments and therefore reduce waiting time		
		Alignment of working days and hours with neighboring countries at border crossings	2	Provides avenue to expedite crossing of shipments and therefore reduce waiting time		
		Alignment of formalities and procedures with neighboring countries at border crossings	2	Provides avenue to expedite crossing of shipments and therefore reduce waiting time		
	Transit facilitation	Transit facilitation agreement(s) with neighboring country(ies)	2	Reduction in time spent at the border	2	Efficient transit agreements and risk assessments lead to fewer delays and improved response to supply chain disruptions.

continued next page

Table: *Continued*

Group	Subgroup	Measure	SUSTAINABILITY: Impact on Mitigating GHG Emissions		RESILIENCE: Impact on Enhancing GVC Resilience	
			Low-1/ Mid-2/ High-3	Possible Channel	Low-1/ Mid-2/ High-3	Possible Channel
General Trade Facilitation	Transit facilitation	Customs authorities limit the physical inspections of transit goods and use risk assessment	2	Reduction in time spent at the border		Efficient transit agreements and risk assessments lead to fewer delays and improved response to supply chain disruptions.
		Supporting pre-arrival processing for transit facilitation	2	Reduction in time spent at the border		
		Cooperation between agencies of countries involved in transit	2	Reduction in time spent at the border		
Digital Trade Facilitation	Paperless trade	Automated Customs System (e.g., ASYCUDA)	3	Reduction in waiting time; Elimination of printed papers; Elimination of physical delivery	3	Digitalization directly contributes to GVC resilience by enabling real-time tracking and reducing dependency on physical processes.
		Internet connection available to customs and other trade control agencies at border-crossings	2	Indirect, but enabler		
		Electronic single window system	3	Reduction in waiting time; Elimination of printed papers; Decrease in the number of procedures involved; Lesser trips required to comply with requirements		
		Electronic submission of customs declarations	3	Reduction in waiting time; Elimination of printed papers; Elimination of physical delivery		
		Electronic application and issuance of import and export permit	3	Reduction in waiting time; Elimination of printed papers; Elimination of physical delivery		
		Electronic submission of sea cargo manifests	3	Reduction in waiting time; Elimination of printed papers; Elimination of physical delivery		

continued next page

Table: *Continued*

| Group | Subgroup | Measure | SUSTAINABILITY: Impact on Mitigating GHG Emissions | | RESILIENCE: Impact on Enhancing GVC Resilience | |
			Low-1/ Mid-2/ High-3	Possible Channel	Low-1/ Mid-2/ High-3	Possible Channel
Digital Trade Facilitation	Paperless trade	Electronic submission of air cargo manifests	3	Reduction in waiting time; Elimination of printed papers; Elimination of physical delivery	3	Digitalization directly contributes to GVC resilience by enabling real-time tracking and reducing dependency on physical processes.
		Electronic application and issuance of Preferential Certificate of Origin	3	Reduction in waiting time; Elimination of printed papers; Elimination of physical delivery		
		E-payment of customs duties and fees	3	Reduction in waiting time; Lesser trips required to comply with requirements		
		Electronic application for customs refunds	3	Elimination of printed papers; Lesser trips required to comply with requirements		
	Cross-border paperless trade	Laws and regulations for electronic transactions are in place (e.g., e-commerce law, e-transaction law)	2	Enable the shift from manual to electronic processes.	3	Digitalization directly contributes to GVC resilience by enabling real-time tracking and reducing dependency on physical processes.
		Recognized certification authority issuing digital certificates to traders to conduct electronic transactions	2	Help facilitate the use and boost confidence on the security of electronic transactions		
		Electronic exchange of customs declaration	3	Reduction in waiting time; Elimination of printed papers		
		Electronic exchange of certificate of origin	3	Reduction in waiting time; Elimination of printed papers		
		Electronic exchange of sanitary and phytosanitary (SPS) certificate	3	Reduction in waiting time; Elimination of printed papers; Reduce cargo storage time		
		Paperless collection of payment from a documentary letter of credit	3	Reduction in waiting time; Elimination of printed papers		

continued next page

Table: *Continued*

Group	Subgroup	Measure	SUSTAINABILITY: Impact on Mitigating GHG Emissions		RESILIENCE: Impact on Enhancing GVC Resilience	
			Low-1/ Mid-2/ High-3	Possible Channel	Low-1/ Mid-2/ High-3	Possible Channel
Sustainable Trade Facilitation	Trade facilitation for SMEs	Trade-related information measures for small and medium-size enterprises (SMEs)	2	Lesser trips required to comply with requirements; Reduction in paper use	2	SME inclusion in trade facilitation measures and digital access promotes diversified and agile GVC participation, enhancing resilience.
		SMEs in Authorized Economic Operators (AEO) scheme (i.e., government has developed specific measures that enable SMEs to more easily benefit from the AEO scheme)	3	Allow qualified SMEs to benefit from preferential measures like rapid release times, fewer physical inspections, and reduced documentary requirements.		
		SMEs access single window (i.e., government has taken actions to make single windows more easily accessible to SMEs, e.g., by providing technical consultation and training services to SMEs on registering and using the facility.)	3	Reduction in waiting time; Elimination of printed papers		
		SMEs in a national trade facilitation committee (i.e., government has taken actions to ensure that SMEs are well-represented and made key members of national trade facilitation committees)	1	Ensures coordination of various stakeholders for seamless implementation of trade facilitation.		
		Other special measures for SMEs	1	Other measures may include reduction in inspection and paperwork for a specific minimum shipment value.		
	Agricultural trade facilitation	Testing and laboratory facilities available to meet SPS of main trading partners	2	Decrease in the number of procedures involved	2	Streamlined certification and special treatments for perishable goods ensure the continuity of agricultural trade under various conditions.

continued next page

Table: *Continued*

Group	Subgroup	Measure	SUSTAINABILITY: Impact on Mitigating GHG Emissions		RESILIENCE: Impact on Enhancing GVC Resilience	
			Low-1/ Mid-2/ High-3	Possible Channel	Low-1/ Mid-2/ High-3	Possible Channel
Sustainable Trade Facilitation	Agricultural trade facilitation	National standards and accreditation bodies are established to facilitate compliance with SPS	2	Reduction in cargo storage time; Decrease in the number of procedures involved	2	Streamlined certification and special treatments for perishable goods ensure the continuity of agricultural trade under various conditions.
		Electronic application and issuance of SPS certificates	3	Reduction in waiting time; Elimination of printed papers		
		Special treatment for perishable goods at border-crossings	3	Reduction in waiting time; Reduce risk of spoilage		
	Women in trade facilitation	Trade facilitation policy/ strategy to increase women's participation in trade	1	Information on trade procedures and requirements are accessible to women to reduce burdensome procedures.	1	Inclusive policies increase the diversity of stakeholders in GVCs, leading to broader perspectives in risk management and innovation.
		Trade facilitation measures to benefit women involved in trade	1	Trade facilitation measures, like use of digital tools, can ease customs transactions of women entrepreneurs.		
		Women membership in the national trade facilitation committee or similar bodies	1	Membership of women in committees can help in women's participation in the implementation of trade facilitation measures		

Source: Authors based on Kim et al. (2024).

REFERENCES

Asian Development Bank (ADB). 2021. *Global Value Chain Development Report: Beyond Production*. Manila. https://www.adb.org/publications/global-value-chain-development-report-2021.

———. 2023. 2023 Trade Finance Gaps, Growth, and Jobs Survey. ADB Briefs. No. 256. https://www.adb.org/sites/default/files/publication/906596/adb-brief-256-2023-trade-finance-gaps-growth-jobs-survey.pdf.

ADB and United Nations Economic Commission for Asia and the Pacific (ESCAP). 2021. *Asia-Pacific Trade Facilitation Report 2021: Supply Chains of Critical Goods Amid the COVID-19 Pandemic: Disruptions, Recovery, and Resilience*. Manila: ADB. https://www.adb.org/sites/default/files/publication/737991/asia-pacific-trade-facilitation-report-2021.pdf.

Al Zeyoudi, T.A., et al. 2023. Sustainable Trade Forum Panel Discussion: Strengthening Sustainable Supply Chain Resilience: Navigating Global Disruption. 28th Conference of Parties. United Arab Emirates. https://unfccc-events.azureedge.net/COP28_94542/agenda.

Anderson, J., and E. Van Wincoop. 2004. Trade Costs. *Journal of Economic Literature*. 42 (3). pp. 691–751. https://www.aeaweb.org/articles?id=10.1257/0022051042177649.

Ashcroft, S. 2023. Top 10 Disruptive Supply Chain Tech. Supply Chain. https://supplychaindigital.com/top10/top-10-supply-chain-technologies.

Association of Southeast Asian Nations (ASEAN). 2021. ASEAN Adopts Framework for Circular Economy. News. 21 October. https://asean.org/asean-adopts-framework-for-circular-economy/.

Automated System for Customs Data (ASYCUDA). 2020. Sri Lanka Trade Facilitation Reforms. https://asycuda.org/wp-content/uploads/2020/ASYCUDA%20Compendium%202020%20-%20Sri%20Lanka.pdf.

ASYCUDA. 2022. ASYCUDA Compendium 2022: Digital Connectivity for Inclusive Trade. Geneva: United Nations. https://asycuda.org/wp-content/uploads/ASYCUDA-Compendium-2022-Timor-Leste-1.pdf.

Bair, J. 2005. Global Capitalism and Commodity Chains: Looking Back, Going Forward. *Competition and Change*. 9 (2). pp. 153–180. https://www.researchgate.net/publication/228339509_Global_Capitalism_and_Commodity_Chains_Looking_Back_Going_Forward?enrichId=rgreq-18579edcfdb172329ab5e768af7883ad-XXX&enrichSource=Y292ZXJQYWdlOzIyODMzOTUwOTtBUzoxMDY0OTUxMjc1ODg4NjhAMTQwMjQwMTgyNTg3Ng%3D%3D&el=1_x_3&_esc=publicationCoverPdf.

Barrientos, S. 2014. Gender and Global Value Chains: Challenges of Economic and Social Upgrading in Agri-Food. *EUI Working Paper* No. 2014/96. https://cadmus.eui.eu/bitstream/handle/1814/32897/RSCAS_2014_96.pdf.

Barrientos, S., G. Gereffi, and A. Rossie. 2021. Economic and Social Upgrading in Global Production Networks: A New Paradigm for a Changing World. *International Labour Review*. 150. pp. 3–4. https://www.researchgate.net/publication/228278108_Economic_and_Social_Upgrading_in_Global_Production_Networks_A_New_Paradigm_for_a_Changing_World?enrichId=rgreq-414ca2db526fec16bec02d0c2b707c33-XXX&enrichSource=Y292ZXJQYWdlOzIyODI3ODEwODtBUzo3MjQ3NzQ2ODI2NTI2NzJAMTU0OTgxMTE1ODI2Ng%3D%3D&el=1_x_3&_esc=publicationCoverPdf.

Beheshtinia, M.A. and M. Fathi. 2022. Energy-Efficient and Sustainable Supply Chain in the Manufacturing Industry. https://www.diva-portal.org/smash/get/diva2:1739321/FULLTEXT01.pdf.

Blumenschein, F., et al. 2017. Fostering the Sustainability of Global Value Chains (GVCs). https://www.global-solutions-initiative.org/wp-content/uploads/2022/11/Trade_Fostering-the-Sustainability.pdf.

Borchert, I., et al. 2017. Services Trade Protection and Economic Isolation. *World Economy*. 40 (3). pp. 632–652. https://onlinelibrary.wiley.com/doi/abs/10.1111/twec.12327.

Business Continuity Institute (BCI). 2020. The Future of Supply Chain. https://www.thebci.org/
        static/7324b815-9364-47d3-9277ab4ce9aa4c0f/a3e39af5-193d-428d-b603d3cf7e600f39/BCI-
        0007d-The-Future-of-Supply-ChainSingles-Low.pdf

———. 2023. *BCI Supply Chain Resilience Report 2023*. https://www.sgs.com/en/-/media/sgscorp/
        documents/corporate/brochures/sgs-kn-bci-supply-chain-resilience-report-2023-sponsored-by-sgs-
        en.cdn.en.pdf.

Dai, T.T. 2021. Environmental Impact of Trade Facilitation in Vietnam: An Assessment of Trade in
        Environmental Goods. Masteral thesis, Ritsumeikan Asia Pacific University. https://ritsumei.repo.
        nii.ac.jp/?action=repository_action_common_download&item_id=15263&item_no=1&attribute_
        id=20&file_no=1.

Decker, C., et al. 2008. Cost-Benefit Model for Smart Items in the Supply Chain. *The Internet of Things*. pp.
        155–172. https://link.springer.com/chapter/10.1007/978–3–540–78731–0_10.

Deng, X., et al. 2008. GIS-based Traceability System of Agricultural Product Safety.
        https://www.researchgate.net/publication/292865141_GIS-based_traceability_system_of_
        agricultural_product_safety.

Dong, H. 2021. The Impact of Trade Facilitation on the Networks of Value-Added Trade – Based on Social
        Network Analysis. *Emerging Markets Finance and Trade*. 58 (8). pp. 2290–2299. https://www.
        tandfonline.com/doi/abs/10.1080/1540496X.2021.1974393.

Duval, Y. and S. Hardy. 2021. A Primer on Quantifying the Environmental Benefits of Cross-Border Paperless
        Trade Facilitation. *ARTNeT Working Paper Series*. No. 206. May. Bangkok: ESCAP. https://www.unescap.
        org/kp/2021/primer-quantifying-environmental-benefits-cross-border-paperless-trade-facilitation.

Ellen MacArthur Foundation. 2019. Completing the Picture: How the Circular Economy Tackles Climate
        Change. 2021 Reprint. https://emf.thirdlight.com/file/24/cDm30tVcDDexwg2cD1ZEcZjU51g/
        Completing%20the%20Picture%20-%20How%20the%20circular%20economy%20tackles%20climate%20
        change.pdf.

Engman, M. 2005. The Economic Impact of Trade Facilitation. *OECD Trade Policy Papers*. No. 21. Paris: OECD
        Publishing. https://www.oecd-ilibrary.org/docserver/861403066656.pdf?expires=1701402020&id=id
        &accname=guest&checksum=DF717F05750B7FC2C4A7EE86C3442B7A.

Escaith, H. 2017. Accumulated Trade Costs and Their Impact on Domestic and International Value Chains.
        Chap. 4 in *Measuring and Analyzing the Impact of GVCs on Economic Development*. Washington, DC:
        World Bank.
        http://www.worldbank.org/en/topic/trade/publication/global-value-chain-development-report-
        measuring-and-analyzing-the-impact-of-gvcs-on-economic-development.

Economic and Social Commission for Asia and the Pacific (ESCAP). 2015. *Asia-Pacific Trade and Investment
        Report: Supporting Participation in Value Chains*. Bangkok: UNESCAP. https://www.unescap.org/sites/
        default/files/Full%20Report%20-%20APTIR%202015.pdf.

ESCAP. n.d. Framework Agreement on Facilitation of Cross-Border Paperless Trade in Asia and the Pacific.
        https://www.unescap.org/projects/cpta.

Ferrantino, M. 2012. Using Supply Chain Analysis to Examine the Costs of Nontariff Measures (NTMs) and the
        Benefits of Trade Facilitation. *World Trade Organization (WTO) Economic Research and Statistics Division
        (ERSD) Working Paper* 2012–02. Geneva. https://doi.org/10.2139/ssrn.2006290.

Gani, A., 2017. The Logistics Performance Effect in International Trade. *The Asian Journal of Shipping and
        Logistics*. 33 (4). pp. 279–288.

Gebhardt, M., et al. 2022. Increasing Global Supply Chains' Resilience after the COVID-19 Pandemic: Empirical
        Results from a Delphi Study. *Journal of Business Research*. 150. pp. 59–72.

Geng, M., S.A. Mansouri, and E. Aktas. 2017. The Relationship between Green Supply Chain Management and Performance: A Meta-Analysis of Empirical Evidences in Asian Emerging Economies. *International Journal of Production Economics*. 183 (A). pp. 245–258. https://www.sciencedirect.com/science/article/pii/S0925527316302870.

Govindan, K., et. al. 2015. Lean, Green and Resilient Practices Influence on Supply Chain Performance: Interpretive Structural Modelling Approach. *International Journal of Environmental Science and Technolology*. 12. pp. 15–34. http://www.bioline.org.br/pdf?st15002.

Halaszovich, T.F., and A. Kinra. 2020. The Impact of Distance, National Transportation Systems and Logistics Performance on FDI and International Trade Patterns: Results from Asian Global Value Chains. *Transport Policy*. 98. pp. 35–47.

Hamprecht, J. et al. 2005. Controlling the Sustainability of Food Supply Chains. *Supply Chain Management: An International Journal*. 10 (1). pp. 7–10. https://www.researchgate.net/publication/242019661_Controlling_the_Sustainability_of_Food_Supply_Chains.

Helble, M. and B. Shepherd. 2017. *Win-Win: How International Trade Can Help Meet the Sustainable Development Goals*. Manila: ADB. https://www.adb.org/publications/win-win-how-international-trade-can-help-meet-sdgs.

Hummels, D. and G. Schaur. 2013. Time as a Trade Barrier. *American Economic Review*. 103 (7). pp. 2935–2959. https://www.aeaweb.org/articles?id=10.1257/aer.103.7.2935.

Ibrahim, R. L. and K. B. Ajide. 2020. Trade Facilitation, Institutional Quality, and Sustainable Environment: Renewed Evidence from Sub-Saharan African Countries. *Journal of African Business*. 23 (2). pp. 281–303. https://www.tandfonline.com/doi/full/10.1080/15228916.2020.1826886.

Iftikhar, A., et al. 2022. Digital Innovation, Data Analytics, and Supply Chain Resiliency: A Bibliometric-Based Systematic Literature Review. *Annals of Operations Research*. pp. 1–24.

International Energy Agency (IEA). 2022. *Global Supply Chains of EV Batteries*. Paris: IEA. https://www.iea.org/reports/global-supply-chains-of-ev-batteries.

International Monetary Fund (IMF). 2022. *World Economic Outlook: War Sets Back the Global Recovery*. https://www.imf.org/en/Publications/WEO/Issues/2022/04/19/world-economic-outlook-april-2022.

International Renewable Energy Agency (IRENA). 2021. *Renewable Power Generation Costs in 2021*. Abu Dhabi. https://www.irena.org/publications/2022/Jul/Renewable-Power-Generation-Costs-in-2021.

International Transport Forum (ITF). 2021. ITF Transport Outlook 2021. https://www.oecd-ilibrary.org/transport/itf-transport-outlook-2021_16826a30-en.

Jacobi, S. 2024. Resilient Supply Chains: Yesterday, Today, and Tomorrow. Hinrich Foundation. https://www.hinrichfoundation.com/research/article/sustainable/resilient-supply-chains/.

Jones, L., M. Demirkaya, and E. Bethmann. 2019. Global Value Chain Analysis: Concepts And Approaches. *Journal of International Commerce and Economics*. US International Trade Commission. https://www.usitc.gov/publications/332/journals/concepts_approaches_in_gvc_research_final_april_18.pdf.

Kalaiarasan, R.,et al. 2022. The ABCDE of Supply Chain Visibility: A Systematic Literature Review And Framework. *International Journal of Production Economics*. 248. p. 108464. https://www.sciencedirect.com/science/article/pii/S0925527322000573.

Kaplinsky, M. and R. Morris. 2014. Developing Industrial Clusters and Supply Chains to Support Diversification and `Sustainable Development of Exports in Africa - The Composite Report. https://www.researchgate.net/publication/275518116_Developing_Industrial_Clusters_and_Supply_Chains_to_Support_Diversification_and_Sustainable_Development_of_Exports_in_Africa_-_The_Composite_Report.

Kim, K., et al. 2023. The Role of Trade in Asia and the Pacific's Net Zero Pathways: Overview and Policy Implications. *ADB Briefs*. No. 274. November. Manila: ADB. https://www.adb.org/sites/default/files/publication/927166/adb-brief-274-trade-asia-pacific-net-zero-pathways.pdf.

Kim, K., S. Basu-Das, and Z. Ardaniel. 2024. Trade Facilitation and Climate Change Nexus. Manuscript.

Krishnan, A., V. De Marchi, and S. Ponte. 2022. Environmental Upgrading and Downgrading in Value Chains: A Framework for Analysis. *Economic Geography*. 99 (1). pp. 1–26. https://www.researchgate.net/publication/362666870_Environmental_Upgrading_and_Downgrading_in_Global_Value_Chains_A_Framework_for_Analysis?enrichId=rgreq-d18c052ad0a09db35c370f1fb4ecdf64-XXX&enrichSource=Y292ZXJQYWdlOzM2MjY2Njg3MDtBUzoxMTQzMTI4MTA4MTcwMzU0MEAxNjYxODY1NzAyND Uy&el=1_x_3&_esc=publicationCoverPdf.

Li, Y., et al. 2022. The Impact of Green Technology Innovation on Global Value Chain Upgrading in China's Equipment Manufacturing Industry. *Frontiers in Environmental Science*. 10. p. 1044583. https://www.frontiersin.org/articles/10.3389/fenvs.2022.1044583/full.

Lucas, B. 2021. Impacts of Trade Facilitation on Carbon Emissions. *K4D Helpdesk Report*. 976. Brighton, UK: Institute of Development Studies. https://www.gov.uk/research-for-development-outputs/impacts-of-trade-facilitation-on-carbon-emissions.

Lund, S., et al. 2020. Risk, Resilience, and Rebalancing in Global Value Chains. Report prepared by McKinsey Global Institute. https://www.mckinsey.com/capabilities/operations/our-insights/risk-resilience-and-rebalancing-in-global-value-chains.

Malacrino, D., A. Mohommad, and A. Presbite. 2022. Global Trade Needs More Supply Diversity, Not Less, IMF Blog. 12 April. https://www.imf.org/en/Blogs/Articles/2022/04/12/blog041222-sm2022-weo-ch4#:~:text=Though%20trade%20flows%20have%20adjusted%2C,than%20during%20previous%20global%20crises.

Martínez-Zarzoso, I. 2023. Trade Facilitation and Global Value Chains in a Post-Pandemic World. *ADBI Working Paper*. 1378. Tokyo: Asian Development Bank Institute. https://doi.org/10.56506/YUCF1465.

Memedovic, O.,et al. 2008. Fuelling the Global Value Chains: What Role for Logistics Capabilities?. *International Journal of Technological Learning, Innovation and Development*. 1 (3). pp. 353–374.

Moise, E. and S. Sorescu. 2015. Contribution of Trade Facilitation Measures to the Operation of Supply Chains. *OECD Trade Policy Papers*. No. 181. Paris: OECD Publishing. https://www.oecd-ilibrary.org/trade/contribution-of-trade-facilitation-measures-to-the-operation-of-supply-chains_5js0bslh9m25-en.

Mubarik, M.S., et al. 2021. Resilience and Cleaner Production in Industry 4.0: Role of Supply Chain Mapping and Visibility. *Journal of Cleaner Production*. 292. p. 126058.

Musyoki, J. 2020. Simplifying Trade Processes for Kenya Competitiveness. Trade Information Portal Forum, 35th UN/CEFACT Webinar. https://unece.org/fileadmin/DAM/cefact/cf_forums/2020_October_Geneva/PPTs/7Oct_2-3-Musyoki-Kenya.pdf.

Natasha, M.H., S. Lim, and Y. Duval. 2021. Assessing the Environmental Impact of Trade Procedures: A Case Study of the Export Process of Bangladesh Readymade Garments. *Trade, Investment and Innovation Working Paper Series*. No. 02. December. Bangkok: ESCAP. https://www.unescap.org/kp/2021/assessing-environmental-impact-trade-procedures-case-study-export-process-bangladesh

North American Research Partnership. 2019. Quantifying Emission Reduction, Queue Reduction, and Delay Reduction Benefits from the Nogales Unified Cargo Processing Facility: Final Report for the Border 2020 Program, April 2019. North American Research Partnership; T. Kear Transportation Planning and Management, Inc.; and Crossborder Group.

Organisation for Economic Co-operation and Development (OECD). 2018. *Trade Facilitation and the Global Economy*. Paris: OECD Publishing. https://www.oecd-ilibrary.org/trade/trade-facilitation-and-the-global-economy_9789264277571-en.

Rupa, R.A., and A.N.M. Saif. 2021. Impact of Green Supply Chain Management (GSCM) on Business Performance and Environmental Sustainability: Case of a Developing Country. *Business Perspectives and Research*. 10 (1). pp. 140–16. https://journals.sagepub.com/doi/pdf/10.1177/2278533720983089.

Saslavsky, D. and B. Shepherd. 2012. Facilitating International Production Network: The Role of Trade Logistics. *World Bank Policy Research Working Paper*. No. 6224. Washington, DC: World Bank. https://papers.ssrn.com/sol3/papers.cfm?abstract_id=2160675.

Schröder, U. 2008. Challenges in the Traceability of Seafood. *Journal of Consumer Protection and Food Safety*. 3. pp. 45–48. https://link.springer.com/article/10.1007/s00003-007-0302-8.

Schwellnus, C., A. Haramboure and L. Samek. 2023. Policies to Strengthen the Resilience of Global Value Chains: Empirical Evidence from the COVID-19 Shock. *OECD Science, Technology and Industry Policy Papers*. No. 141. Paris: OECD Publishing. https://doi.org/10.1787/fd82abd4-en.

Shepherd, B., 2022. Modelling Global Value Chains: From Trade Costs to Policy Impacts. *The World Economyo*. 45 (8). pp. 2478–2509. https://developing-trade.com/wp-content/uploads/2021/07/Working-paper-DTC-2021-1.pdf.

Sirimanne, S. and R. Adhikari. 2022. Vanuatu Shows How to Reduce Emissions Through Trade Facilitation.

Takpara, M.M., C.F. Djiogap, and B. Sawagodo. 2023. Trade Policy and African Participation in Global Value Chains: Does Trade Facilitation Matter? *Journal of Economic Integration*. 38 (1). pp. 59–92. https://www.jstor.org/stable/27197638.

Tamiotti, L., et al. 2009. Trade and Climate Change: A Report by the United Nations Programme and World Trade Organization. Geneva: WTO. https://www.wto.org/english/res_e/booksp_e/trade_climate_change_e.pdf.

United Nations (UN). 2021. Asia Pacific Trade and Investment Report 2021: Accelerating Climate-Smart Trade and Investment for Sustainable Development. https://www.unescap.org/sites/default/d8files/knowledge-products/APTIR2021_3.pdf

Wang, Z., S.-J. Wei, and K. Zhu. 2013. Quantifying International Production Sharing at the Bilateral and Sector Levels. *NBER Working Paper* No. 19677. (Revised 2018.) https://www.nber.org/papers/w19677. https://openknowledge.worldbank.org/server/api/core/bitstreams/96dcdf6c-5fb1-51e9-b17b-4210caf01767/content.

World Economic Forum (WEF). 2021. Digital Traceability: A Framework for More Sustainable and Resilient Value Chains. September. https://www3.weforum.org/docs/WEF_Digital_Traceability_2021.pdf.